MOBILE MANSIONS

Courtesy Win Howard

MOBILE MANSIONS

TAKING "HOME SWEET HOME" ON THE ROAD

Douglas Keister

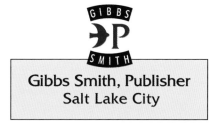

GIBBS P SMITH

Gibbs Smith, Publisher
Salt Lake City

To Forrest and Jeri Bone and
the Tin Can Tourists who honor
the past to better the future.

First Edition
10 09 08 07 06   5 4 3 2 1

Text © 2006 Douglas Keister
Photographs © 2006 Douglas Keister except as noted

Published by
Gibbs Smith, Publisher
P.O. Box 667
Layton, Utah 84041

Orders: 1.800.748.5439
www.gibbs-smith.com

Designed by Steve Rachwal
Printed and bound in Hong Kong

Library of Congress Cataloging-in-Publication Data
Keister, Douglas.
  Mobile mansions : taking "home sweet home" on the road /
Douglas Keister.— 1st ed.
     p. cm.
  Includes bibliographical references.
  ISBN 1-58685-773-8
  1. Recreational vehicle living. I. Title.

TX1110.K443 2006
796.7'9—dc22

2005030721

CONTENTS

6

THE ROMANCE OF THE ROAD

43

CAMP CARS AND HOUSE CARS

69

CAMPERS AND VANS

91

BUS CONVERSIONS

107

MOTORHOMES

135

PERSONAL VISIONS

154

ACKNOWLEDGEMENTS

158

SUGGESTIONS FOR FURTHER READING

159

RESOURCES

THE ROMANCE OF THE ROAD

Americans are a restless people. We seem to have a wandering gene plugged into our DNA. After all, we are a nation of immigrants, born of social and political unrest. Even the Native Americans who gingerly welcomed us were, for the most part, nomadic people, content to follow the seasons or the buffalo. We Americans always seem to be looking for greener pastures and wondering what's over the next hill. Even the more sedentary of us find ways to express our wandering spirit. Indeed, inert folks, who seem to be permanently moored in their Barcaloungers, aren't content with a few channels on their televisions. They want dozens or even hundreds. Psychologists tell us to stop and smell the roses. Sure, we tell them, as long as we can be looking up the varieties of roses in our guidebooks while calling our friends on our cell phones to tell them how great they smell.

One of the best places to experience this restless, wandering spirit in action is on the nation's roads where millions (yes, millions) of recreational vehicle enthusiasts crisscross freeways, state highways, and dusty country roads. The size of their transporters range from diminutive pop-up tent trailers to diesel-belching, lumbering leviathans complete with hot tubs, balconies, and gourmet kitchens. Judging by the number of motorhomes, trailers, truck campers, and private buses on our nation's highways in recent years, especially compared with twenty or thirty years ago, it's easy to think that "RVing" is a relatively recent phenomenon. While it is certainly true that there are more modern-day gypsies than ever before, the phenomenon of hitting the road with a tidy little home on wheels has a long, rich history.

Mobile mansions are, for many, the greatest expression of our right of liberty. This right of liberty, which legal scholars translate as the freedom of movement, is spelled out in the

An early home on wheels makes its way across Nevada's Black Rock Desert during a 1996 re-creation of the trek along the Applegate Trail. The trail, which was established in 1846 and wound up in Oregon, was one of the first trails used by emigrants as they made their way west in search of a better life. Photograph © Jess Smith.

Declaration of Independence. Indeed, the most quoted phrase in that treasured document is, "We hold these truths to be self-evident, that all men are created equal, that they are endowed by their Creator with certain unalienable Rights, that among these are Life, Liberty and the pursuit of Happiness." Most Americans also know Patrick Henry's famous demand, "Give me liberty, or give me death!"

While it's true that Americans seem to have a wandering spirit and relish the idea of exercising their liberty, it is only in the past century that the common person has been able to fully exercise that right. We may like to point to great explorers like Lewis and Clark, Kit Carson, and Daniel Boone; outdoor enthusiasts like Henry David Thoreau and John Muir; and the great western migrations of the nineteenth century as proof of our wandering ways, but the truth is, until the advent of the automobile, the vast majority of Americans rarely ventured more than a few miles from their home.

INTO THE WEST

The exploration and development of America was driven by people, many of whom, like the Gypsies (see pages 8–11), were fleeing persecution and looking for a better way of life. A country as geographically large as the United States necessitated a lot of moving around. The longest and most celebrated of these migrations were the wagon trains that made their way west in the nineteenth century. Families packed up their meager belongings and loaded them into the covered wagon, a classic American-made trailer. The Studebaker Company, which would become a major manufacturer of automobiles some years later, produced the most popular of the covered wagons, the Conestoga. The emigrants' wagons became rolling homes for months during their long, arduous journey west. Even after their arrival in the promised land, their petite mobile homes served as a shelter until more permanent homes could be constructed. For most Americans though, their wandering days were through. Aside from an occasional train trip, most people stayed put. Primitive roads and an agrarian lifestyle kept them down on the farm. Americans may have had the freedom of movement, but few had the means to exercise it. That would soon change.

THE GYPSIES

Living on the road is a temporary affair for most folks. Whether on vacation or traveling between jobs, living in a home on wheels is something people do for a break, except for one group, the Gypsies. Historians tell us that the original Gypsies were a nomadic people whose origins were in India. The name *Gypsy* comes from a misunderstanding of where they were from. Accounts differ, but either by design or mistake the Gypsies were thought to have come from Egypt, and they generally made no great effort to correct the error. Around the year 1000, groups of them reached modern Turkey and Greece, and by 1300 they were well established in central Europe. In the next few centuries, they spread all over Europe and eventually to America. Most lived on the road for extended periods of time, which necessitated bringing their homes along with them. As nomads, they became very adept at living on the road. As a result of their social customs and tribal life, they rarely tried to assimilate into the culture of the country they inhabited. Much of their nomadic lifestyle developed as a result of the persecution they endured wherever they went.

The public has a fractious relationship with these migratory people. On one hand, they are seen as rootless, uncommitted, non-taxpaying hustlers, while on the other they are viewed as a people who truly exemplify the joys of an unshackled lifestyle that embraces the ability to pick up and leave for greener pastures at a moment's notice. The truth, of course, is somewhere in the middle. In the late nineteenth century, it became all the rage in Great Britain for well-to-do folks to purchase a fancy gypsy wagon and go on gypsy outings. When automobiles replaced the gypsy wagons, these outdoor forays became known as autogypsying. In the twenty-first century, the old gypsy caravans have become highly collectible and sell for substantial amounts of money.

The horse-drawn gypsy wagons may be no more, but thanks to James Nelson, folks can have a modern-day version. James has created over a dozen gypsy wagons, some of which are mounted on conventional vans, while others are stand-alone trailers. All of them are true to the gypsy spirit and have real stained-glass windows, rich wood interiors, and whimsical detailing. These two caravans, glowing with dozens of candles, were photographed at a Tin Can Tourists rally in Camp Dearborn, Michigan.

The interior of the Gypsy caravan is all aglow thanks to a generous supply of votive candles.

Wealthy Romany folk and the occasional non-Romany British eccentric commissioned elaborately decorated wagons. This example, built by Dunton and Sons of Reading, Berkshire, is known as a Reading wagon. Dunton, a premier builder of gypsy wagons, operated from the 1870s until 1922. This restored example dates from 1918. Photographed at Glasgow Museum of Transportation with permission of Glasgow Museums, Glasgow, Scotland. Background photographed at Iona, Scotland.

The interior of a typical gypsy caravan is a study in well-thought-out simplicity but with artistic and colorful embellishments. On the far left and almost out of view is a cast-iron stove that doubles as a heater. A lantern-top roof with clerestory windows provides ample illumination and headroom. There are lots of storage cabinets. A ladder that can be used to access high cabinets and provide egress into the caravan is also visible. This gypsy wagon, dating from around 1900, was acquired in France in 1954. It can be seen at Pioneer Village, Minden, Nebraska.

Gypsy wagons are still being used in some rural locations. This trio was photographed in the lush farmland of the Cotswolds near Cheltenham, England. Photograph © Brian Coleman.

Until the advent of the automobile, just about the only people traveling and living on the road were the Gypsies. This group was photographed in Bethesda, Maryland, in 1888 by Frances Benjamin Johnston. Courtesy Library of Congress.

As the twentieth century dawned, sweeping social changes occurred that gave Americans the opportunity to move around when and where they wanted. The development of mechanized farming, which led many people to find jobs in the cities; the concurrent push for an eight-hour workday; and, more importantly, vacations gave Americans something they had rarely experienced: free time. Teddy Roosevelt extolled the virtues of an outdoor lifestyle and established national parks for all to enjoy. Americans yearned to escape the noisy, smoky, dirty cities to experience the wonder of the great outdoors. But, how to get there? Transportation by horse and buggy was too slow, and the cost of train travel, meals, and lodging was beyond the means of most Americans. Even if people could afford train travel, folks had to limit themselves to where the trains went and the schedules they kept.

Aficionados of the bicycle accomplished the first tentative forays beyond the cities. These two-wheeled marvels enabled people to go places on their own schedule and without a draft animal to tend to. Certainly these journeys were of no great length, but they helped to whet the appetite for bigger things to come.

THE AUTOMOBILE

At the beginning of the twentieth century, the horseless carriage, a newfangled mode of transportation, emerged on the scene. These motorized contraptions promised to allow people to move around at will without regard to a train's schedule or a draft animal's care and feeding. Because of the high cost of automobiles, they were primarily playthings of the wealthy. Well-to-do vehicle owners had a huge impact on the lives of ordinary citizens since their lives and exploits were well documented in the popular press. Soon newspapers, magazines, and books were filled with images of people clad in their Sunday best bumping down the road in their

Camping off the beaten path was an arduous undertaking requiring a rugged constitution and roadworthy clothing. The care and feeding of draft animals was another challenge that hampered outdoor travel for all but the most hardy individuals. Even well-to-do folks, who could afford to have others tend to the animals, seldom ventured far beyond the places trains went. This group of adventurers, portrayed on a stereo-scope card published by Underwood and Underwood in 1902, was photographed in California's Yosemite Valley. Note the ample clothing, particularly on the women. At that time, even in the wilderness, women were expected to adhere to certain rules of decorum. Courtesy Library of Congress.

The New York to Paris Around the World race was celebrated, albeit with considerable artistic license, in the 1965 motion picture The Great Race, *starring Tony Curtis as Leslie Galant III, Jack Lemmon as Professor Fate, and Natalie Wood as suffragette Maggie Dubois. Four loose interpretations of the Thomas Flyer were created for the movie.*

fanciful machines. The usually tranquil countryside was invaded by noisy, rattling, smoke-belching automobiles painted in wild colors and piloted by bespectacled adventurers. Babies cried, animals bolted, and farmers raised their fists and shouted, "Get a horse," but there was no turning back. The age of the automobile with all of its joys, wonderment, and problems had arrived. There would be no turning back.

The automobile enabled the traveling public to experience a new kind of freedom. In an article titled "Gregarious and Individual Transportation" in the May 1910 issue of the *American Motorist* magazine, the writer decried the mixed blessings of the railroads and the advantages of traveling by automobile: "The individual has had to sacrifice much of his liberty of action to take advantage of

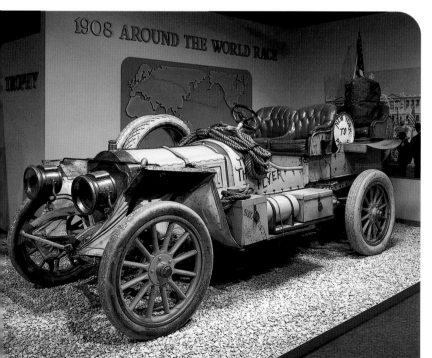

Before there were manufactured camp cars and accessories, people who wanted to go on automotive adventures had to lash all of their equipment to their vehicles. That phenomenon is illustrated well in this 1907 Thomas Flyer, built by the E. R. Thomas Motor Company in Buffalo, New York. This one-of-a-kind vehicle was the winner of the New York to Paris race in 1908. Prior to the race, the Thomas Flyer was outfitted with extra gas tanks, tires, and camping gear. The 169-day race spanned 13,341 land miles plus about 9,000 sea miles. George Schuster, the only crewmember to travel the entire distance, drove the car into Paris on July 30. Second place went to the Germans who arrived twenty-six days later. Photographed at the National Automobile Museum (the Harrah Collection), Reno, Nevada.

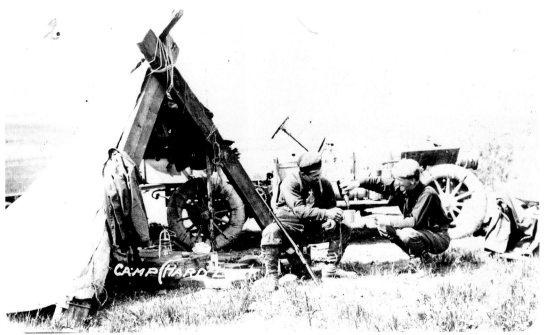

[the railroad]. He must go with the crowd at the time the crowd wants to go and by the route the crowd takes." The writer goes on to amplify his point that breaking away from the crowd and motoring down the road in an automobile represents a type of freedom worth striving for.

Early-day automobile enthusiasts were at first content to motor around their local area and return at night, but before long some of the more adventurous souls decided to go on longer excursions. These forays beyond the city limits, though exciting, were fraught with problems. Many roads were little more than trails and even well-established roads were deeply rutted with wagon-wheel tracks. Add a little bit of rain and they became impassable muddy bogs. Still, the intrepid motorists persisted. Getting from Point A to Point B was the stuff of adventure, no matter if the distance was a few miles or hundreds of miles. Once these motor pioneers had conquered the roadways, they were presented with another problem—where would they lie their heads down for the night? Unlike today, when thousands of motels, campgrounds, courts, and hotels line the highway, at the turn of the nineteenth century, there was only one viable choice: the hotel.

THE TYRANNY OF HOTELS

Once motorized argonauts finally made it into town, they needed to figure out a place to stay. While some stayed with friends and family, many had to stay in hotels. Typical lodging choices at the time were large big city hotels, hotels associated with vacation areas, and "drummers" hotels (so called because the bulk of their clientele were traveling salesmen who drummed up sales). The road-weary motorists had the easiest time fitting in at the hotels in vacation areas. They no doubt generated a fair amount of interest when they pulled up in their motorcars. But their arrival at the big city hotels and the drummers hotels was another matter. Hotels had a strict set of rules and customs, and at every juncture someone had their hand out for a tip.

Most hotels had a large number of regular guests, and many hotels had the feel of a men's club. This was especially true at the drummers hotels where upwards of 90 percent of the guests were regulars. Before even getting to the front desk, a guest had to run the gauntlet of baggage men, bellhops, and doorkeepers all expecting a tip. Finally, a guest had to deal with the hotel clerk, an individual who wielded incredible power. The clerk determined if there was a room available and often even set the price. It was considered bad manners to ask for the price before committing to stay at the hotel. These complicated interactions were strictly a male domain. If a wife accompanied her husband, she was to sit demurely in an area off the main lobby and let her husband make all the arrangements. If a woman was traveling alone or with another woman, well, that was just not in keeping with hotel policy. Women like that had to find more appropriate accommodations elsewhere.

In the early days of autocamping, manufacturers of beds for automobiles capitalized on the fact that they were more affordable than buying a tent or staying in a hotel. Auto beds came in a variety of configurations from hammocks that were suspended over the seats, boards that spanned the seats, and this six-foot spring bed that must have required some modification of the automobile's seats. The advertisement appeared in the March 1924 issue of Outdoor Life *magazine.*

If a person was lucky enough to secure a reasonable room, the problem of where to eat had to be addressed next. In smaller towns, the hotel often possessed the only public eating place and once again hands were out expecting a tip to secure a good table. The gustatory offerings were often far from sumptuous. It seems that the regular guests were meat-and-potatoes men, and the restaurants catered to them. Even when there were other places to eat, guests were essentially forced to eat at the hotel's restaurant since many of them operated on the American plan, where the price of the room included two meals. What were the motorists to do?

AUTOCAMPING PROVIDES THE SOLUTION

Human beings have a long tradition of confronting and overcoming obstacles, and motor enthusiasts were going to find a way to enjoy their automobiles to the fullest. Inadequate roads, uncertain lodging, and unappetizing food weren't going to keep them from exercising their liberty for long. To solve the lodging problem, they strapped canvas tents and lean-tos to their automobile's running boards and loaded their backseats with the kids, a variety of food packed in tin cans, and canteens full of water. It wasn't long before savvy entrepreneurs, taking note of the autocamping phenomenon, started making all manner of camping accessories for cars, including stoves, folding furniture, and portable-washing equipment. For those who didn't want to bother with a tent, companies like the Outers Equipment Company of Chicago made contraptions that turned the car's seats into a bed. "Snap your fingers at the grasping hotel man," said the Outers ad that snubbed the hotels. "Take a Foldaway Bed along and sleep in your car."

But what about the common person? Sure it was great to read about the motoring adventures of the elite, but how could the average citizen experience the things he or she

Most early camp cars were playthings of the wealthy. T. Coleman du Pont, president of E.I. Du Pont de Nemours and Company, funded a paved highway in Delaware, which later became U.S. 13. Around 1911, he commissioned a camping vehicle so he could inspect the roadwork. His camping car had a Stoddard-Dayton chassis fitted with a delivery truck body, which was modified for camping. The car included a horsehair-stuffed mattress, cook stove, ice box, roll-down curtains, and storage spaces for utensils and supplies. When extra sleeping room was needed, twin silk tents could be attached to the vehicle's sides. Courtesy Library of Congress.

"RedSeal" Auto Bed

THE nationally known Auto Bed for use either in a tent at the side of the car or as an extra cottage bed. When closed, rolls to a bundle 6 inches by 47 inches. Erected more quickly than any other Auto Bed. No loose pins or nuts to get misplaced. Sag and stretch-proof. Open size is 47 inches wide and 6 feet 4 inches long. It is strictly high grade, but very *cheap* in price.

"RedSeal" PalmetTent

A surprisingly large and roomy one-pole tent, made of guaranteed waterproof closely woven duck. Entire top of two thicknesses. Three thicknesses at the corners and other vital points. Insect, reptile, and wind-proof. Open size 11 feet by 9 feet, folds and packs into a 48-inch by 10-inch packing bag.

Schaefer Tent and Awning Co.
1421 Larimer Street, Denver, Colorado
We are Exclusive Manufacturers of "Red Seal" Camp Equipment

FREE: Large catalogue and low price list No. 404 describing fully all of the latest styles of Auto Tents and other camp out goods.

When autocamping made the transition from fad to mainstream mania, there were plenty of manufacturers poised to advertise their wares. Tents, lean-tos, and cots suddenly became auto tents, motor tents, and auto beds. The Schaefer Tent and Awning Company of Denver, Colorado, offered a variety of auto tents, auto beds, and even a motorcycle tent in this advertisement that appeared in the March 1924 issue of Outdoor Life magazine.

had read about? The solution would come from a revolutionary product offered by Henry Ford called the Model T, the first automobile that was truly available and affordable. Almost overnight Americans took to the road with camping supplies lashed to their Tin Lizzies (so named because, at the time, hard-working female servants were called Lizzies and, in Canada, horses were sometimes called Lizzies). This more down-to-earth breed of people was actually better equipped to embrace the idea of autocamping, with its ideal of sleeping outdoors and cooking over an open fire than the more wealthy element. After all, many commoners had grown up in rural areas where people had to rely on their own ingenuity to get through the trials and travails of a typical day. This first burst of using the automobile as a motorized covered wagon was also referred to as auto gypsying since many of its aesthetics were aligned with the traditional gypsy images of families enjoying the outdoors, sitting around a campfire, and moving from place to place at will.

A number of other factors helped the autocampers to become an American institution. First and foremost was the improvement of the roads. Although there were three million miles of roads compared to three hundred thousand miles of railway line, most of the roads were dirt, which in inclement weather rendered them virtually impassable. That began to change in 1916 when President Woodrow Wilson signed the Federal Roads Act, which appropriated $75,000,000 for the improvement of post roads. Another factor was the war, which was raging in Europe. Well-do-do folks found their plans to vacation in Europe seriously curtailed. These folks looked for adventures stateside and autocamping appealed to the more adventurous of them. Those two factors got an added boost when an unlikely group of well-known men decided to try their hand at autocamping. Their well-documented adventures fueled the autocamping craze.

This photograph, taken in Porterville, California, in 1920, depicts a very early house car. Records indicate that the vehicle, which appears to be a Pierce Arrow truck, was probably first registered in 1915. The body is undoubtedly handcrafted and was probably constructed sometime in the late teens. Befitting the motoring style of the times, the men's and women's garments are more than a little substantial, and thus provide a buffer against the dust and the bumps of the road. The photograph depicts three generations of a California family—Carrie E. (Hunt) Bacon with her father-in-law, T. L. Bacon, and her niece. The driver/cook is also in the photo. Courtesy Virginia Coffman.

THE VAGABONDS

In 1914, Henry Ford and Thomas Edison took their families on a vacation to the Florida Everglades. By all reports, it was an enjoyable trip. The two wealthy industrialists found the outdoor experience relaxing, providing them time to recharge their internal batteries. Then in 1915, tire-magnate Harvey Firestone joined the duo on a motor trip from Los Angeles to San Diego. The group enjoyed the experience so much that Edison proposed doing a "gypsy" trip during the following summers at which time they would actually camp together. To enhance the outdoor experience, noted naturalist John Burroughs was invited along. Although Burroughs' name is not well known today, at the time he was a respected spokesman and essayist who advocated a more nature-oriented lifestyle. On the surface, Burroughs was an unlikely member of the group since he was decidedly anti-industrial.

Henry Ford described Burroughs in an interview with a reporter:

> He detested money and especially he detested the power which money gives to vulgar people to despoil the lovely countryside. He grew to dislike the industry out of which money is made. He disliked the noise of the factories and railways. He criticized industrial progress, and he declared the automobile was going to kill the appreciation of nature.... So I sent him an automobile with the request that he try it out and discover for himself

whether it would not help him to know nature better. That automobile—and it took him some time to learn how to manage it himself—completely changed his point of view. He found that it helped him to see more, and from the time of getting it, he made nearly all of his bird-hunting expeditions behind the steering wheel. He learned that instead of having to confine himself to a few miles around Slabside [Burroughs' home in West Park, New York], the whole countryside was open to him. Out of that automobile grew our friendship, and it was a fine one.

From 1913 until Burroughs' death in 1921, Ford kept him supplied with automobiles.

During the years of the vagabonding adventures, a number of other movers and shakers of the early twentieth century joined the expeditions, including President Warren

The Vagabonds didn't always rough it. In this photograph, taken on August 30, 1918, the entourage leaves the comfortable Hamilton Hotel in Hagerstown, Maryland. The vehicle is a right-hand drive 1917–18 Buick. Henry Ford sits gloomily in the backseat, no doubt irritated that the photographer caught him in one of his competitor's vehicles. Courtesy Norm Brauer.

In an era when bridges were few and far between, numerous ferries dotted the river ways of America. In this photograph taken during the Vagabonds' 1918 excursion, three of the vehicles prepare to leave a ferry on the Jackson River in Virginia. The lead vehicle, carrying Edison (left side of the front seat), is a 1916–17 Packard, which may explain the less-than-cheery expression on Ford's face (right side of the backseat). Courtesy Norm Brauer.

Harding, E. G. Kingsford (a lumberman whose name became associated with Kingsford Charcoal), Methodist bishop William F. Anderson, and an assortment of mayors, politicians, and industrialists. Of equal importance were the members of the media who were always alerted when an expedition was to take place. Ford and Edison, in particular, were consummate showmen who knew how to publicize their companies and their activities. Everywhere the Vagabonds went the newspapermen followed with their notebooks and cameras. Every activity from what they ate, to who could fell a tree the quickest (octogenarian Burroughs won that contest), to how they shaved (Edison used a car's rearview mirror), to their choice of clothing was well documented by the press.

In truth the Vagabonds were hardly roughing it— they were accompanied by dozens of support staff and Firestone even brought his butler along. Nevertheless, Burroughs was a bit frustrated in his attempts to get his fellow campers to fully embrace the outdoor life. At one point, he commented that while he was admiring a beautiful flowing stream, Edison and Ford were calculating the flow of the stream to determine how much energy it could produce.

In the end, thanks to their celebrity status and the reports filed by the media, the three titans of industry and the scraggly naturalist helped elevate autocamping to national obsession. By the end of the Vagabonds' trips in 1924, the public had embraced autocamping with gusto.

The Vagabonds frequently posed for photographs for the ever-present media. This photograph, taken in 1918, depicts (left to right) Edison, Burroughs, Ford, and Firestone at the Old Evans Mill near Leadmine, West Virginia. Courtesy University of Akron, Ohio.

A full complement of vehicles loaded down with furniture, tents, food, cooking equipment, and an entire staff to attend to the Vagabonds' needs followed along like a motorized wagon train. Add the ever-present reporters and photographers and the expeditions took on a circus-like atmosphere.

Pictured here is the 1922 Lincoln kitchen truck used on some of the later expeditions. The truck was loaded down with a supply of food, staples such as steaks, ham, bacon, vegetables, eggs, milk, and cream that were purchased along the way from farmers. Local people frequently dropped by the camp with gifts of home-baked goods and fresh fruits and vegetables. One camp employee was assigned to go into town for a special bread that had been baked for Henry Ford. The group enjoyed noonday meals and generous rest periods at pleasant wayside areas that were the precursors of today's roadside table parks. The 1922 Lincoln was photographed in the garage at Fair Lane, the Henry Ford Estate in Dearborn, Michigan. A White truck that carried tents and equipment for the Vagabonds is on display at the Henry Ford Museum.

This photograph, taken in Michigan during one of the Vagabonds' last camping trips, circa 1923, depicts (left to right) Henry Ford, charcoal magnate E. G. Kingsford, and Edison with their wives. The empty chair (a common memorialization device at the time) is for John Burroughs who died in 1921. The 1923 trip may have been one of the last for the Vagabonds, but their well-publicized excursions spurred a national obsession with motorized camping that continues to this day. Courtesy Henry Ford Estate, Dearborn, Michigan.

The Vagabonds went all out when their camp was visited by persons with even loftier stations in life than the titans of industry. This photograph depicts chefs Fisher and Herman preparing a meal on July 23, 1921, at Camp Harding in Pectonville, Maryland. Camp Harding got its temporary name from President Warren G. Harding who spent time traveling with the Vagabonds. Courtesy Norm Brauer.

The Tin Can Tourists, founded in 1919, grew into a formidable autocamping organization within a few short years. This postcard, dating from the late 1920s, depicts the frenetic activity of a TCT camp in Gainesville, Florida. Courtesy Milton Newman collection.

THE TIN CAN TOURISTS

Human beings are social animals. We tend to seek out like-minded fellows. Thus, it wouldn't be long before autocampers found other autocampers. The first cohesive groups of these neo gypsies were people who journeyed to Florida in the winter to escape the harsh weather in the rest of the country. As early as 1916, little clutches of campers were gathering together around Tampa. Some came in horse-drawn peddler's carts, others in touring cars with tents strapped to the running boards, and still others in one-of-a-kind camp cars made of wood bodies bolted to car and truck frames. By 1919, there were enough of these folks gathered in one spot to form an organization. By the end of the year, the Tin Can Tourists organization was established, complete with a royal sergeant, also known as the Mayor of Easy Street (the main street in the camp); an emblem (a tin can soldered to the radiator cap of a member's car); and a list of goals (including high moral values, wholesome entertainment, and a safe and clean camping area). The Tin Can Tourists took their name from the tin can provisions that they subsisted on and, some say, also from the Tin Lizzies many of them drove.

Word of the organization spread rapidly. In 1921, there were over eighteen hundred members. Thousands more joined every year. In 1936, fifteen hundred rigs showed up at a single rally in Sarasota, Florida. In 1938, there were thirty thousand members, and, by 1963, there were one hundred thousand members. Over the years, the Tin Can Tourists were staunch defenders of their members and their lifestyle.

As with all organizations, schisms developed between members who wanted the organization to be more expansive and those who wanted it more exclusive. The most notable feud was between the exclusionary white-pants Willies and the members who wanted the organization to be open to as many people as possible. The white-pants Willies dared suggest that the office of Royal Can Opener be changed to the office of the Royal Chief. They also wanted the soldered tin-can emblem dropped for a spiffy diamond-shaped emblem that cost $0.50, a pricey accessory when most folks struggled to make a few dollars a day. Eventually the white-pants Willies broke away from the Tin Can Tourists and formed the Automobile Tourist Association.

By the 1930s, the name Tin Can Tourists had become part of the nation's vocabulary, and almost everyone who owned a trailer or house car was called a Tin Can Tourist whether they were a member or not. Articles in newspapers spoke of Tin Can Tourist encampments, Tin Can Tourists invasions, and even the Tin Can Tourists problem since it was widely perceived that thanks to these drifters America would turn into a nation of rootless, wandering motorists who wouldn't pay taxes or contribute to communities.

The Tin Can Tourists were organized in 1919 in Tampa, Florida. Like most successful groups, they experienced growing pains and schisms developed between different groups of members. By the 1930s, the ATA (Automobile Tourists Association) became a rival organization. When the ATA split with the TCT, the group took the TCT's logo design, bylaws, and even their motto. Eventually both clubs' memberships dwindled, but in 1998 Forrest and Jeri Bone resurrected the Tin Can Tourists as an organization for owners of vintage trailers and motor coaches.

THE HEYDAY OF THE HOUSE CAR AND CAMP CAR

Early photographs of Tin Can Tourists' encampments in the 1920s depict gatherings of vehicles where the dominant vehicle is a boxy little home on wheels. These house cars and camp cars differ from auto camps since they are fully self-contained vehicles. Camp cars are typically vehicles that support tents and awnings. They are specifically designed for camping and usually have a tent or awning attached. House cars are self-contained and can be said to be the true predecessor of the modern-day motorhome.

Fueled by tales of the motor camping adventures of the Vagabonds, individuals constructed all manner of house and camp cars. Most were built directly on a truck or car frame, while others were adapted from existing truck bodies. There were also a few companies that manufactured camp and house cars. Owners usually furnished a vehicle, and the company removed the car's or truck's body and replaced it with their own creation. Most notable among these were the

One of the most popular series of children's adventure books was the long string of forty Tom Swift books that were published between 1910 and 1941. The books, which were written by a number of authors under the pseudonym Victor Appleton, always revolved around protagonist Tom Swift's adventures that involved technology and transportation. The transportation subjects ranged from motorcycles, cars, dirigibles, airships, submarines, tanks, locomotives, to even house cars. In Tom Swift and His House on Wheels, published in 1929, Tom builds a huge four-room house car with two bedrooms, a kitchen, and a living room. The whole apparatus was powered by a 12-cylinder engine.

On the car's maiden voyage to the Mountain of Mystery, an adventure ensues when Tom encounters the bad guys. He and his chum Ned Newton save the day and in the end the house on wheels serves as a honeymoon cabin after Tom marries longtime girlfriend Mary Nestor. Ever thoughtful, Tom positioned the kitchen at the rear of the vehicle so Mary could cook while the vehicle was in motion. "Putting the kitchen in the rear insures the odors being carried away as the machine moves along," explained Tom.

No motor camper's satchel would be complete without maps and guidebooks. An illustration of two young women preparing a meal, graces the cover of the 1926 edition of Motor Camping. A stylish 1926 Packard Touring Car is in the background. The book contains chapters on saving money while motor camping, equipping your car for camping, and general information about the outdoor life. There is even a chapter titled Camping with a Ford, since around 50 percent of automobiles on the road in 1926 were Fords. Over half of the book's 380 pages are devoted to lists of motor camps and campgrounds throughout the United States.

Of particular note is the chapter on primitive camping, which specifies how a couple of "husky fellows" need take little more than a flivver and some ingenuity on a motor camping expedition. Advice is given on how to boil water without a pot as well as the joys of eating cattails, blue flower water lilies, acorns, and Jerusalem artichokes. For the more carnivorously minded, instructions are provided on how to capture, prepare, and cook muskrats, which, according to the book, taste every bit as good as squirrel.

In the early 1920s, Mr. and Mrs. William H. Morgan were ready to take their ministry wherever they felt the need via their Boston-based Little Church on Wheels (founded in 1920). According to their brochure, they held free open-air gospel meetings every evening. Employing the latest technology, they used a Power Magnavox Amplifier hooked up to a Graphophone for musical accompaniment. On Sundays, the amplifier was used to enhance radio broadcasts. The tower and its electric cross were collapsible, which was necessary as early roadways had low bridges and underpasses.

Lamsteed Kampkar mounted on a Model T body (see pages 44–45) and the Zagelmeyer Kamper Kar mounted on a Ford, Reo, or Chevrolet body (see pages 46–49).

With all these assorted homes on wheels traversing the countryside, individuals and municipalities eventually began to take notice. Civic leaders considered providing a place for motor tourists in their communities. They reasoned that motor tourists might as well get their supplies in their towns, so the communities could reap the rewards. Before long, thousands of autocamps peppered the countryside, small towns, and big cities. Estimates indicate that there were between three and six thousand autocamps in the United States in the early 1920s. Some municipalities, hoping to cash in on the local trade, operated free camps, while others charged a modest fee. The largest of these camps was Denver's Overland Park, which opened in 1915. This 160-acre motor camping metropolis boasted accommodations for over two thousand motor campers. Perhaps an even better measure of the allure of the automobile and motor camping was that in 1921 approximately twenty thousand hardy folks drove across the country while only nine years before, a scant twelve people made the trip.

As the Roaring Twenties turned into the depressive thirties, the house car took back-seat to that other icon of mobile America, the travel trailer.

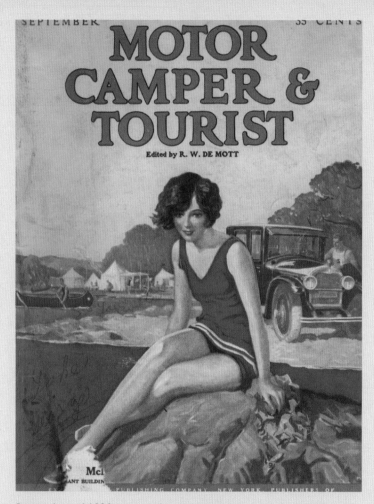

During the mid-1920s, auto and motor camping was popular enough to claim its own monthly magazine, Motor Camper and Tourist. The destination-oriented magazine also had articles on camp etiquette, the latest motor camping accessories, a question-and-answer section, jokes, and even a primer on the use of radios (the publisher also produced a radio magazine). Courtesy Stapleton Library, Indiana University of Pennsylvania.

An article in the September 1924 issue of Motor Camper and Tourist magazine is devoted to an autocamping expedition along the Pacific Northwest's portion of the old Oregon Trail. Most automobiles that were adapted for camping made ample use of the vehicle's running boards to secure tents and food storage boxes and iceboxes. Note the bottle of milk that was, no doubt, secured locally and the child's bed suspended above the front seat. Courtesy Vince Martinico collection.

The benefits of fresh air and exercise are ably illustrated in this photograph from the September 1925 issue of Motor Camper and Tourist magazine. Courtesy Indiana University of Pennsylvania collection.

Camping Cars on Tour

—A quartet of New York men who
going to cross the country in a re-
ded auto. Leon Schwab, of New York
Leon Hormark, of Poughkeepsie,
York; James P. Ireland, of New York
and Edward C. Remson, of Larch-
mont, N. Y.

r Right—Rear-Admiral John Watson
the Orange Free State with his sleep-
and touring-car on his trip through the
, paying a visit to Holland. Mr.
on is travelling only for the purpose
ving education to his children, as he
"Travelling in the world means
education."

—Bishop Edward Fawcett of the
opal Diocese of Quincy, Ill., with his
nd daughter, Miss Susanne Fawcett,
cliffe College Senior, are spending the
er in a completely equipped home on
s touring New England. The camp
eels contains everything from running
ater and a bathtub to a writing table
kitchenette. The family were photographed arriving at Boston.

Three different camp cars are illustrated in this September 1924 issue of Motor Camper and Tourist magazine. Of particular note is the special platform for the canine sentinel that was making a trip across the United States. Courtesy Vince Martinico collection.

Specialty magazines like Motor Camper and Tourist were essentially preaching to the choir about the virtues of camping with an automobile. The bulk of its display advertisements concentrated on items, including portable radios, convenience foods, and tools, that were intended to enhance the autocamping experience. More mainstream outdoor-oriented magazines like Outdoor Life were awash with advertisements for camp cars, auto tents, and auto beds. Outdoor Life touted itself as the "National Authority on Automobile Camping" and "the First Magazine with an Autocamping Department." For a few issues in the late 1920s, the magazine even adjusted its name to Outdoor Life Outdoor Recreation. Normally a he-man magazine with a cover that had illustrations of manly men stalking and slaying wild beasts, this June 1928 issue displayed a softer side with an illustration of a happy autocamping couple.

THE GOLDEN AGE OF THE TRAILER

House cars and camp cars were, to be sure, expensive items. One major problem was what to do with them when a person wasn't camping. A lot of people were still somewhat content to strap their camping gear to their automobile and head off on an adventure. But it wouldn't be long before someone mounted a folding tent to an old artillery trailer and the first camping trailer was born. In the 1920s, there were numerous manufacturers of pop-up tent trailers advertising their wares in outdoor-oriented magazines. But the seminal moment occurred in the summer of 1928 on a family vacation.

Indiana bacteriologist Arthur Sherman took his family camping in the northern woods of Michigan that year. Sherman brought along one of the most up-to-date tent trailers. The family arrived in a driving rainstorm and the process of erecting the tent, which was supposed to take no more than ten minutes, turned into a nightmarish experience. Vowing to find a better way, Sherman returned to his Indiana home and sketched a simple design for a hard-sided trailer that needed no setting up. He gave his diagram to a carpenter and awaited the results. His children dubbed the boxy affair the Covered Wagon. When Sherman returned to northern Michigan the following summer, he was besieged by his fellow campers who wanted a closer look at the Covered Wagon. The proverbial light bulb went off, and Sherman, hoping for a few sales, took his creation to the Detroit Auto Show in January 1930. He came back

In 1934, a young couple purchased plans and hardware from the Hammer Blow Tool Company and built this trailer for their honeymoon. Like many trailers from the early 1930s, the Hammer Blow was essentially home built. Manufacturers supplied the basic items like wheels, axles, frames, and hitches, and do-it-yourselfers, following plans supplied by the manufacturer, did the rest. The tow car pictured is a 1936 Oldsmobile that was produced by the onetime General Motors division based in Lansing, Michigan. Photographed in Newcastle, California. Courtesy Vince Martinico collection.

In the 1930s, the travel trailer ruled the highways. This boom time for travel trailers was fueled by the Great Depression, which uprooted Americans; a prediction by Wall Street financial guru Roger Babson that one out of two Americans would be living in a trailer in twenty years; and vastly improved highways. Understandably, travel trailers and travel in general were the subjects of magazine and newspaper articles, movies, and even comic postcards.

with 118 orders for his homely little trailer. Thus, the Covered Wagon Trailer Company was born. It was the first commercially produced hard-sided trailer that was affordable for the masses. By 1935, the Covered Wagon Trailer Company was very profitable. It had become America's largest trailer manufacturer, no small feat in the midst of the Great Depression.

Sherman's Covered Wagon was certainly a milestone in trailer history, but the most significant event that fueled the trailer boom in the '30s was a statement by a man named Roger Babson. He had predicted the stock market crash in 1929 and had become something of a financial guru during the '30s, not unlike Warren Buffet or Alan Greenspan are today. In 1935, Babson predicted that one out of every two Americans would be living in a trailer within twenty years. Babson's influence was so enormous that his prediction fueled a huge trailer boom. Within a short period of time, there were hundreds of trailer manufacturers churning out trailers as fast as they could for what they perceived would be a huge demand. Babson's prediction, of course, never came to pass, but within a few years America was awash with trailer manufacturers, trailer magazines, movies that featured trailers, celebrities endorsing trailers, and books that extolled the virtues of the mobile lifestyle. There were also negative stories in the media that complained about rootless gypsies in their rolling bungalows not paying taxes and filling up city parks with their trailers and trash—hence the term *trailer trash*. The late '30s also saw the emergence of comic trailer postcards. These brightly colored cards featured three dominant subjects: the virtues of the carefree trailer lifestyle and the comic adventures that ensued, scantily clad lovelies and leering men, and the outhouse since trailer bathrooms were not standard amenities. Alas, by the late '30s, a supply of trailers that far exceeded the demand, the dark clouds of war, and finally the war itself put the brakes on the golden age of the travel trailer.

HOUSE CARS OF THE 1930S

Although the trailer dominated the mobile American market, some notable house cars were produced in the 1930s. Continuing the tradition started in the 1920s, there were still plenty of home-built boxy house cars in the '30s. Because of the Great Depression, many of these home-built vehicles served as semipermanent residences as people moved around looking for jobs. The Great Depression also fueled the return of the idea of sleeping in your car, but unlike the romantic notion of sleeping in your car in the early years, in the '30s it was often a necessity. Autocamping during this time looked more like the opening credits of *The Beverly Hillbillies*, with all of a family's possessions (including granny) strapped to the car than the happy-go-lucky images of jolly families in search of adventure of a few years earlier.

Streamline design came into its own in the 1930s, and nowhere was it more noticeable than in automotive design. In 1934, the first mass-produced streamlined car, the Chrysler Airflow (also called the Desoto Airstream), was manufactured. Prior to the Airflow, motoring journalist and aviator William B. Stout built a vehicle in 1932 that looked like a giant legless cockroach that Stout dubbed the Scarab. In 1934, Austrian-born designer Alexius Pribil sketched out and later fabricated a teardrop-shaped house car called the Aircar (see page 63). Around the same time, futuristic architect Buckminster (Bucky) Fuller along with Starling Burgess and Anna Biddle designed the Dymaxion car. Three of the vehicles, which were intended to be adaptable to a number of uses, including a transporter and even a house car, were built during 1933 and 1934. Alas, they were too advanced for the times and never went into production. This sole survivor, Dymaxion #2, was photographed at the National Automobile Museum (the Harrah Collection), Reno, Nevada.

Despite this rather grim reality, the 1930s was also the era of airplanes, streamlining, and Buck Rogers. Some rather innovative automobiles and house cars took their cue from these modernistic icons, and visionary manufacturers introduced futuristic designs. Among the more interesting designs were those of motion picture cameraman John Roy Hunt who built a handful of streamline house cars (see pages 61–63); industrial designer Brooks Stevens who built a combination house car/mobile laboratory for the Racine, Wisconsin-based company S. C. Johnson and Son (see page 60); and the Thompson Raise the Roof Four-Sleeper and Diner Cabin Sedan made by southern California inventor and watchmaker Arthur J. Thompson in 1934 (see pages 56–57). Even architect Buckminster Fuller got into the streamlined vehicle act with his Dymaxion Car, which could serve as a car, van, transporter, or, with the right accessories, a home on wheels.

THE POSTWAR ERA

During World War II, the production of nonessential items, which included travel trailers and house cars, was seriously curtailed. Except for trailers that were commissioned by the government for temporary housing and a few one-of-a-kind units, very few were produced during the war years. All of that changed quite rapidly after the end of World War II. Almost immediately after the conflict was over, trailer manufacturers infused with a new supply of raw materials dusted off their old equipment and geared up for production. Some companies that produced airplanes during the war now turned their sights to the burgeoning recreation market and started producing streamline trailers using the tooling they had used to manufacture aircraft. Companies that wished to make house cars had a slightly slower time getting started since automobile designs now favored a more integrated body and simply removing the automobiles existing body and replacing it with a house car body was not quite as easy as it used to be.

THE RETURN OF THE CAMP CAR

After four long years of war, the boys returned home and promptly married and started families. Family life was back in vogue and that meant family vacations. Budgets, of course, were tight for these freshly minted families, and camping was a reasonable alternative to motels and hotels. As trailer manufacturers struggled to meet demand, families adapted and rediscovered the camp cars of years past, this time under the guise of that quintessential suburban icon the station wagon. The station wagon's folding seats made it ideal for sleeping. Just throw in some folding chairs, a cookstove, and an ice chest, and voilà, the family had a tiny mobile home. Automobile manufactures touted the adaptability of their station wagons to suit every use with camping at the top of the list. A number of companies like Sears and Roebuck, J.C. Penney, and Western Auto followed suit with lines of camping equipment tailored specifically to station wagons. Even the traditional family sedan was adapted by a few companies into a camper-friendly vehicle. Notable among these were the Nash, which offered a model with a double bed that fit into the backseat and trunk area, and the Kaiser, which had a cleverly articulated truck lid and fold-down seats that converted the car for sleeping and hauling equipment and supplies.

Other visionary designers saw a market for some sort of motorized RV and looked for ways to implement their ideas.

BUSES BECOME FAMILY FRIENDLY

One of the first postwar entries into the house car market was made by the Flxible Bus Company, a manufacturer of transit buses. Flxible, which had been making buses since the 1920s, opened up a special Land Cruiser division in 1948 and began making custom bus conversions (see pages 96–99). Other bus-like motor coaches were the Marmon-Herrington (see page 101) and the Victor motor coach, manufactured in Bristol, Indiana, which was built on a GMC chassis. These motor coaches were very pricey and tended to be owned by wealthy individuals or were used by companies to tout their wares in displays on wheels. The most widely known of the traveling displays was General Motors' fanciful Futurliner (see pages 152–53). Bus conversions also became popular with traveling entertainers as a way to transport their equipment and to serve as sleeping quarters when lodging was not available.

In the 1960s and '70s, buses found a new life as personal-statement billboards on wheels and temporary homes for members of the flower power generation. Many of the buses' effervescently colored interiors and eclectic interiors were, no doubt, inspired by a variety of psychotropics that propelled passengers on a different type of journey. Even the mom-and-apple-pie crowd was drawn to the Technicolor transporters as witnessed by the enormous popularity of the television series *The Partridge Family* (1970–74), which featured a brightly painted 1957 Chevrolet school bus.

Bus conversions were bulky and often quite expensive and certainly not for those who wanted a more compact camping experience, but a house on wheels that was affordable arrived with the invention of a clever little device that slid into the bed of a pickup truck.

TRUCK CAMPERS

Home-built truck campers probably existed almost as early as pickup trucks. What can be determined is that by the early 1950s, slide-in truck campers were being manufactured. Three of the earliest truck campers were the Cree Truck Coach, a prototype of which was first exhibited in Chicago in 1945; the Sport King (see pages 72–73), first manufactured in 1949 by Walter King, who was looking for a more sturdy addition to his product line of teardrop trailers; and the Alaskan Camper (see pages 74–76), which had a telescoping roof, and was first manufactured in 1953. Slide-in campers served as an alternative to trailers and motorhomes, since they were easier to maneuver than a trailer and the truck and camper body could be separated when not needed. Slide-in campers have been some of the most popular RVs because of their durability and relative low cost.

Over the years, there have been dozens of manufacturers. Since slide-in campers have to conform to the truck's bed, the configuration remains basically the same on all truck campers, but they come in a variety of lengths. The most basic slide-in campers simply nestle into the truck's bed and are slightly taller than the roof of the truck's cab. Other models extend over the cab to provide a compact sleeping area, while others extend from a few inches to a few feet beyond the rear of the truck to provide additional space. The space beyond the back of the truck is sometimes large enough to wedge in a lilliputian bathroom. The one significant drawback to the truck campers is that the usable space in the camper does not include the cab of the truck. Because there is not egress between the cab and the camper, passengers cannot occupy the camper while it is in motion. This problem is solved with vans.

Slide-in truck campers came into their own in the 1950s and '60s. Their rugged design and compact size offered an alternative for folks who didn't want to drag along a bulky trailer, maneuver a motorhome, or deal with setting up a tent and campsite at every stop. Unlike motorhomes and camping vans, slide-in truck campers could be left at home when not in use. This example, the Dreamer, manufactured by Coons Custom Coach, was available in various lengths and configurations—from a tidy 6½-foot model designed to fit on Jeep-like vehicles, like the International Scout and Ford Bronco, to a 10½-foot model that hung over the back of the pickup. Coons Custom Coach was only one of upwards of fifty camper manufacturers in southern California in 1960. Brochure courtesy Bruce Coons.

Quartzsite, Arizona, is one of the most interesting RV-related places in the world. In the summer, when daytime high temperatures consistently top 110 degrees, the town is only populated by a thousand or so sun-baked souls. But in the winter, hundreds of thousands of snowbirds descend on the arid plain. Originally those who journeyed to Quartzsite in the winter months came for a huge gem show in January, but as the years ticked on Quartzsite became a destination in itself. One of the chief attractions is that much of the land around the town is federal property and administered by the Bureau of Land Management.; camping fees for an entire season hover around $100.

VANS

When thinking of camping vans, the one that usually comes to mind is the sturdy little Volkswagen van. This icon of compact camping can trace its beginnings to the humble and loveable Volkswagen Beetle (known as the Type I), which was on the drawing board as early as the mid-1930s. Executives at Volkswagen saw a market for a larger vehicle and the Volkswagen Van (the Type II) was launched at the Geneva Auto Show in 1949. Almost immediately after the first vans rolled off the assembly line in 1950, people started converting them into campers. By 1951, Volkswagen commissioned a coach company in Westfalia, Germany, to build a camper body and the Volkswagen Westfalia was born. The Volkswagen Van in its Transporter, Kombi, Samba, Micro Bus, and Westfalia configurations became the hippie van of choice in the 1960s and still has strong sales today as the Volkswagen Vanagon.

Seeing the strong sales for the Volkswagen vans, American manufacturers came out with their own versions of camping vans. General Motors announced its plans to build a multipurpose van it dubbed L'Universelle in 1955, but plans were shelved after projections of production costs were higher than expected. By the early 1960s, GM was ready to take another shot at the camper-van market and rolled out three different vans that, like the Volkswagen, had a rear-mounted engine. The GM products were based on the Corvair Car and included the Corvan, the Greenbrier Sports Wagon, and the Greenbrier DeLuxe Sportswagon. From 1961 to 1965, the Greenbrier models were available with camper interiors.

The Ford Motor Company's entry into the camper-van market came in 1961 when mahogany-paneled Kamperkits, complete with a sofa bed, table, ice chest, and Coleman stove were manufactured by Einar Miller of San Bernadino, California, for Ford Econolines. Miller's workers went to Ford dealerships and installed this special-order item. By 1962, Ford also sold a Ford Camper Kit that fit into all of the company's small vans. By 1965, Dodge threw its hat in the ring when it unveiled the camping conversion for its popular Dodge Sportsman Van. The most unique entry in the camper-van market was the Ultra Van (see pages 84–87), made in Hutchinson, Kansas, and powered by a rear-mounted Corvair engine. The whale-shaped van, while never wildly popular, has secured a place in RV history thanks to an enthusiastic group of Ultra Van owners that has formed a club and holds a handful of rallies every year, often in conjunction with the Corvair Society of America (CORSA).

None of the American camper vans was as popular as the Volkswagen. It's unlikely that their combined sales could even hold a candle to Volkswagen's. However, the American companies had bigger things in store.

Enter the motorhome.

KING OF THE ROAD

Home-built, custom-made, and small-production motorhomes have been fabricated almost from the time people hit the road in search of camping adventures, but it wasn't until the 1960s that they became a viable option for the average citizen. The first time the words *motor home* (nowadays most RV enthusiasts combine the two words) were used was in 1958 when Raymond Frank and his teenage son Ronald built a motorized all-weather recreational vehicle for family vacations and called it the Frank Motor Home. With backing from Dodge, their creation was renamed Dodge Motor Home in 1963. It then became the Travco Motor Home in 1965 (see pages 108–109).

Throughout the 1960s, various manufacturers rolled out an array of motorhomes, but most were beyond the reach of average consumers. Then, in 1966, a watershed moment in RV history occurred when a trailer manufacturer in Iowa came out with a boxy little motor-home named the Winnebago (see pages 110–11). Finally, a motorized home on wheels was offered at a price that was affordable for the average person. It doesn't take any great leap of imagination to compare the effect the Winnebago had on the motorhome industry to the effect the Model T had on the automotive industry. The brand Winnebago became synonymous with motorhome.

By the early 1970s, it seems that every automobile and truck manufacturer was trying to hitch their company to the motorhome star. The first couple of years of the '70s were boom times for the industry, and then in 1973 the Arab oil embargo and the ensuing energy crisis almost tripled the price of gasoline overnight, and the production of gas-guzzling motorhomes screeched to an abrupt halt. A number of companies didn't have the resources to weather the energy storm, and they either went bankrupt or restructured. Nevertheless, by the late '70s, the motorhome industry was back on its feet and there hasn't been a significant dip in sales since.

Nowadays most Class A motorhomes have the same boxy bus-like profile, quite simply because it is easier to fit interior elements into a box rather than a curve. This cookie-cutter construction ensures a wide selection of interchangeable interior amenities. The wealth of appliances, cabinets, and electronic gizmos available makes for an almost infinite variety of configurations and can drive the price of a high-end motorhome far beyond $1,000,000. Photographed in Quartzsite, Arizona.

OVER THERE AND ELSEWHERE

The motorhome craze has not been limited to America. In Europe and Australia, thousands of people take to the road on vacations and weekend trips in their caravans (trailers), micro-caravans (small trailers), and campers and campervans (motorhomes). In Australia with its enormous expanses of wilderness, fully equipped motorhomes and smaller vans are particularly popular. Tourists with a desire to get off the beaten path are thrilled to be able to rent a fully equipped motorhome for a more authentic Australian experience. In Europe, and especially in England and Scotland where some of the first trailers were manufactured early in the twentieth century, the roadways are full of tidy homes on wheels, a testament to the enduring spirit of wanderlust. The caravanning activity has been around so long that there are now organizations dedicated to the preservation of antique campers and caravans.

Nowadays, no matter where in the world you reside, there are RVs to fit almost any budget, from diminutive micro vans to lumbering million-dollar McMotorhomes. Whatever their size, they owe their existence to the development and popularization of the automobile and to those individuals who just had to find out what was over the next hill.

What is true about the RVing experience is that there is an amazing camaraderie among its adherents. In many ways, this fellowship harkens back to the days when the pioneers traveled down the road together in search of a better life. Thus, the verse titled *A Song of the Friendly Road,* penned by Tom Withrow and published in *Motor Camping and Tourist* magazine in 1924, is just as meaningful in the twenty-first century as it was back then (see page 40).

The Aussies are particularly fond of motor camping and because of the vast tracts of unpopulated lands, especially in Australia's Outback, fully self-contained RVs are extremely popular. Being lost is merely a temporary inconvenience when one carries all of the conveniences and accoutrements of home. Volvo bus conversion photographed in Victoria, Australia.

Despite frequently gloomy conditions (the Highlands experience measurable rainfall 250 days a year), the Scottish people are avid RVers and many accommodations are open year-round. Caravans (travel trailers) and campervans (motorhomes) often fill the caravan parks to bursting during summer months and on weekends. Photographed at Braidhaugh Caravan Park, Crieff, Scotland.

RVers with upscale tastes have an abundance of options, including luxury RV resorts like Emerald Desert Golf and RV Resort in Palm Springs, California. Emerald Desert boasts 760 spaces with full hookups, an 18-hole golf course, three swimming pools, a mini mart, and numerous other amenities. To ensure its upscale atmosphere, Emerald Desert has a strict "Pride of Ownership" policy, which does not allow tents or tent trailers or any RV less than 19 feet in length.

A SONG OF THE FRIENDLY ROAD

There's many a time on the toilsome road
Of life, where but once we pass,
When a fellow breaks down from an overload
Or finds he's out of gas;
And then, it's up to the man whose bus
Still hits on all six, to help,
And a guy that refuses, or makes a fuss,
Is an ornery sort of whelp.

For the best of men may meet hard luck,
And the best of engines die,
And the best of drivers may fail to buck
Life's hills, that are steep and high;
So never refuse a brother's call,
For only the high gods know
How soon it may be your turn to fall;
How soon you may need a tow.

Oh, life's road is full of ups and downs,
And broken by "thank-you-maams,"
And it's long and lonely between the towns,
So there's need for gracious alms
Of the friendly word, and the human smile,
And the drink, or drop of gas,
That will help him over the last hard mile,
Of the pilgrim we meet and pass.

And perhaps (who knows) when we meet at last,
At the end of the long, long trail,
With the hills and the thank-you-maams all past
There will greet us with joyous hail,
The fellows with whom we've split our gas,
Or helped with a friendly tow,
And they'll give us "a hand" in the friendly land
WHERE ALL GOOD MOTORISTS GO.

—Tom Withrow

On any given day, hundreds of thousands of RVers take to the road in campers, motorhomes, fifth wheels, and vans. Whether it's a weekend outing or a multi-month voyage with no particular destination, RVers are exercising their right to go where they want and when they want. Photographed near Glamis Sand Dunes, California.

CAMP CARS AND HOUSE CARS

It was only a matter of time before early-day autocampers figured out ways to make self-contained campers, eliminating the need for setting up tents or attaching awnings to the vehicle. The first camp cars were home-built units, reflecting the owners' personal needs and also their varied construction skills. The most durable units were built on truck frames that were already engineered for cumbersome loads. It wasn't long before the business community took note of these home-built modern-day gypsy wagons, and a few small companies started building self-contained camp cars, advertising their custom-built units in outdoor- and automotive-oriented publications, like *American Motorist* magazine and *Outdoor Life* magazine.

This 1917 Winton six-cylinder, 48-horsepower house car was custom built by McKay Carriage Works for a southern politician who was running for governor (he lost). The candidate was transported between venues in the house car, and he also gave speeches off the back platform.

The house car eventually made it into the collection of Metropolitan Opera star James Melton and resided on his Connecticut farm for a number of years. In the late 1950s, Melton had to liquidate much of his collection to pay off debts, and Bill Harrah purchased the Winton for his Harrah's Automobile Collection in Sparks, Nevada. Unfortunately, after purchasing the vehicle, Harrah found out that Melton had used the Winton as collateral for one of his numerous loans and the house car was sitting at an impound facility in Massachusetts. Harrah may have had the title, but the sheriff had the Winton. So Harrah consulted his lawyer who informed him that, because of some obscure state's rights law, if Harrah could find a way to get the Winton over the state line to Rhode Island, the vehicle would be his. So Harrah instructed one of his employees to wait until the sheriff's deputy, who was guarding the car, left the facility. Then he told the employee to fire up the engine and drive the ten miles to Rhode Island. The employee seized an opportunity when the deputy went off on an errand, but because the Winton's fuel pump was malfunctioning, the employee had to hand pump the gasoline. The wheezing Winton barely made it to Rhode Island.

In addition to becoming part of Harrah's enormous fourteen-hundred-plus vehicle collection, the Winton served as a registration office during auto shows and swap meets. Automobile collector Buck Kamphausen acquired the vehicle when over twelve hundred of Harrah's vehicles were auctioned off after Harrah's death in 1978. Photographed in Boulder City, Nevada. Background photographed in Quartzsite, Arizona.

The interior of the Winton has been modified during its succession of owners, but its essential character has remained in keeping with the early twentieth century. The fabric-covered walls and ceiling are true to the spirit of a sumptuous railway coach fit for a barnstorming politician. Even the table, which folds down to provide a sleeping area, and chairs are made of quality materials. Two conveniences have been added for the modern-day passenger's comfort: an air conditioner mounted to the ceiling and a small bathroom shoehorned into a closet area (back left side of the picture).

Although there were never a lot of camp car manufacturers (it seems that adventurous folks built their own), they comprise an important chapter in the history of RVing.

The heyday of the camp car was during the 1920s. By that time, autocamping had gone from fad to fashionable thanks in part to the well-publicized autocamping expeditions in the late teens and early twenties by the four Vagabonds (see pages 18–21). Most of the camp cars in the 1920s were automobiles that had been retrofitted with beds and tidy kitchens. By the mid-1920s, autocamping enthusiasts had a publication devoted to their needs called *Motor Camper and Tourist* magazine. By the 1930s, the camp car had evolved into the house car, and many of these units were mounted on sturdy truck chassis.

However, motor camping in the 1930s was ruled by the travel trailer. Travel trailers were much less costly than house cars and had the added advantage of being detachable from the vehicle when in camp. As a result of the Great Depression, those who motor camped could be divided into two distinct groups: those fairly well-to-do folks who camped for pleasure and dispossessed people, particularly migrant workers, who camped in their cars because they had no permanent home.

The camp car returned after World War II, but this time as a pleasure vehicle in the form of the Woody Station Wagon. House cars eventually made a comeback, too, and by the late 1950s they had evolved into another vehicle with a brand new name, the motorhome.

Most early camp cars were custom made by the owner or to the owner's specifications. There were, however, a few firms that advertised production camp cars that were mounted on an automobile chassis. Understandably, the most popular chassis was the economical Ford Model T. One of the premier commercially made camp cars was the Lamsteed Kampcar, designed by Samuel Lambert of St. Louis, Missouri. Lambert is best known because of his namesake, the Lambert Pharmaceutical Company, which manufactured, among other things, Listerine Mouthwash. Lambert was an avid outdoorsman and saw a need for a camp car that was available to the general public at an affordable price. His creation sold for $535, and the advertising claimed that it could be attached to the Model T frame in six hours. Amenities included seating for six, sleeping for four, a folding table, a two-burner stove, an eight-gallon water tank, and ample storage lockers. A complete camping set with camping supplies and eating utensils was also included.

When it came time to put his camp car into full production, Lambert, apparently needing to attend to other duties, turned his creation over to another company based in St. Louis, the Anheuser Busch Company, whose beer-producing operation had been curtailed by Prohibition. During those dry years, Anheuser Busch had turned to manufacturing vehicles, including wagons, truck bodies, and now the Lamsteed Kampcar. Records are a bit sketchy, but the Kampcar was most likely produced from 1915 to 1933, with units manufactured by Anheuser Busch from 1921 to 1931. Its long run is at least partially due to its advertising literature, which celebrated the romance of the road and the virtues of the outdoor lifestyle: "Make this the kind of a vacation you've always dreamed about—enjoy the splendor of Yellowstone, the majesty of the Grand Canyon, visit balmy Palm Beach or the great North Woods. Go anywhere you wish—on your own schedule, over your own railroad system in your own private car, stopping at your own hotel, eating your own cooking at your own table—all in great comfort and at a price you can easily afford."

Only two intact Lamsteed Kampcars are known to exist. This one, mounted on a 1921 Ford Model T, was photographed at the National Automobile Museum (the Harrah Collection), Reno, Nevada.

With awnings rolled up, Lamsteed campers were afforded a sumptuous view while sleeping safely above the ground. Various configurations enabled additional seating, table space, and sleeping accommodations.

CAMP CARS AND HOUSE CARS

Like most house cars of the era, this 1928 Chevrolet House Car was personalized for the owner. This house car's evolution began in 1928 when Clarence Stimpson, an engineer residing in Michigan City, Michigan, purchased a 1928 Chevrolet chassis. Stimpson drew up plans for the interior and exterior woodwork and delivered his drawings and the chassis to the Zagelmeyer Auto Camp Company in Bay City, Michigan.

Zagelmeyer manufactured fold-up camping trailers under the Zagelmeyer De Luxe Auto Camp Trailer name as well as their specialty, the Zagelmeyer Kamper Kar, which was mounted on a Ford coupe or roadster chassis. Zagelmeyer also advertised that they could build custom camp cars for mounting to other types of vehicles, such as a Chevrolet or Reo Speed Wagon. The house car body for the Reo Speed Wagon was 15 feet 6 inches long with a mahogany interior, plush upholstery, wardrobe, drop-down beds, desk/table, and even a sink with running water.

Clarence Stimpson's house car was modeled after the 11 foot 5 inch Gypsy Cruiser's body featured in Zagelmeyer's 1928 catalog. In August 1928, Stimpson, his seventy-nine-year-old father, and another friend took off for California in their new house car Stimpson dubbed the Gypsy, since it was similar to Zagelmeyer's Gypsy model. Their journey to California took them along the Old Spanish Trail, then to Globe, Arizona, and onward to California via the Apache Trail. The reports they mailed home told of a delightful trip and the comforts provided by their house car. They even commented that there were no bad roads, which is testament that all things are relative to one's expectations. After wintering in California, the trio returned to Michigan the following spring.

The house car was stored in Mackinaw City for a time, and then moved to a specially built barn in Roger City where it resided until 1996 when it was acquired by John McMullen of Lapeer, Michigan. McMullen and two friends, Walt Davenport and Gary Callendar, undertook the restoration of the Gypsy, which only had 9,000 miles on it and was in mechanically sound condition. Although the restorers took the entire engine apart, almost all of the work was cosmetic. The biggest challenge was replacing the wooden spoke wheels, which had deteriorated beyond repair. By 1997, the Gypsy was, in the words of John McMullen, "ready for a return trip to California by someone else, not me." Photographed at the Sloane Museum grounds, Flint, Michigan.

One of the most interesting features of the Gypsy Cruiser's interior is the wicker seats, which were used because of their light weight. Curiously, the chairs are not secured to the floor, which must have provided a modicum of excitement when taking turns at anything but the slowest speeds.

In the early days of the automobile, most people used hand signals to indicate when they were stopping or what direction they were turning. Auto manufacturers also came out with a number of inventive devices to facilitate signaling, including directional arrows that flipped up when pulled by a lever. The original owner of the Gypsy had lost his left arm in an accident so he couldn't make the requisite hand signals and, of course, he couldn't pull a lever located on the left side. So an ingenious pulley system was used to activate the left turn signal. The lever, which is attached to a cord and pulleys, is located between the stove and the steering wheel.

Zagelmeyer advertised that its bodies were "a complete five room home on wheels." Depending on which devices were folded up or down, the "rooms" were a dining car, parlor car, cook car, sleeping car, and chair car. The Gypsy Cruiser was marketed with a dark oak interior, black imitation-leather sofa bed, kitchen, and table. In the photograph, the vehicle is configured in the parlor mode, ready to receive guests for a spot of afternoon tea.

Early camp cars were made from just about anything on wheels. Since almost all early vehicles were built with modular parts, it wasn't particularly hard to remove seats, doors, and body panels and replace them with other parts. One company, J. B. Pelletier and Son, a coach builder in Bridgeport, Connecticut, advertised in Outdoor Life magazine that it could build just about anything a customer could dream up. In 1923, Charles Brooks of Cuddbackville, New York, saw the Pelletier advertisement and decided to contact the company.

After some correspondence, Brooks took his 1923 Studebaker Big Six Touring Car along with a sketch of his own design to Pelletier and commissioned the company to convert the Studebaker into a camp car. The creation was dubbed Outdoor Life since that was where Brooks had seen the ad. Brooks and his stepson Stan Hubbard, both avid outdoorsmen, used the car until 1937 when it was put in a barn and stored.

In 1985, Win Howard acquired the camp car from Hubbard. Howard decided to leave the Studebaker in a state of arrested decay as a testament to its rugged beauty.

The interior of the Studebaker camp car is strictly utilitarian. A small table, bed, and folding chairs provide the basic comforts. The vintage linoleum floor covering and the large windows, which afford a spectacular view of the great outdoors within the relative comfort of the vehicle, are worth noting.

In the 1920s, the Zagelmeyer Auto Camp Company was the best-known camp car company. It offered a number of products to suit any budget from the inexpensive tent trailer that was easy to tow to the luxurious Pullman Camping Touring Coach house car.

The Motoring Tourists had a reunion in Arcadia, Florida, in January 1932. True to the style at the time, a number of house cars at the gathering sported personalized and fanciful names, such as Texas Bound and Homette. The Tennessee Traveler pictured on the facing page appears to be the eighth vehicle from the right above. Courtesy Bob and Ann White collection.

The 1920s and early '30s were the heyday of the house car. The Tin Can Tourists, which was established in 1919, had well-attended "conventions" that were jam-packed with house cars and vehicles of all types. Edison, Ford, Burroughs, and Firestone and other celebrities further popularized motor camping and house cars during their well-publicized Vagabonding expeditions. The romance of the road and the much-touted health benefits of the great outdoors lured many Americans to build or purchase one of these tidy homes on wheels. Unfortunately, because of their homemade construction and the maintenance required to keep their engines and drive trains functioning, few house cars have survived.

Bob White knew he had discovered a unique piece of American history when he found this remarkable 1931 Ford AA house car in a barn in Athens, Alabama, where it had been stored for forty years. The roof of the barn had collapsed and bushes and vines, which had grown up around it, had essentially hidden the vehicle from view. But when it was finally extracted from its mooring place, despite being well weathered, everything was intact,

including the engine and interior furnishings. In fact, after cleaning the spark-plugs and adding a bit of lubricant, the engine fired right up.

The bulk of the restoration was executed by Dennis Edwards, who started by doing a basic clean up of the vehicle to assess the general condition. By carefully scraping away the top layer of faded and oxidized paint, Edwards was able to reveal and then copy the original colors. The Tennessee Traveler name is not original but was applied by the current owners, Bob and Anne White, to reflect their home in Pulaski, Tennessee. The naming of a house car follows the practice common during the 1920s and '30s when people often paid homage to their vehicles, lifestyle, and home states with fanciful signage, such as Gypsy, Dunwerkin, Nutshell, Suits Us, Happy Hoosiers, and My Old Kentucky Home. This practice was so widespread that campers often didn't even know each other by their given names and referred to their fellow Tin Can Tourists by names like Mr. Galloping Goose, Mr. Red Rambler, Miss Muncie, and Mrs. Motoroamer. Photographed at the Flywheelers Park, Avon Park, Florida.

The Ford AA's interior was amazingly intact. Although it took a lot of elbow grease, restorer Dennis Edwards was able to refinish the wood without replacing any key elements. The floor is made of rot-resistant redwood planks; the ceiling of tongue and groove oak; and the cabinets of yellow poplar. Accoutrements include a sink, camp stove, potbelly stove, icebox, ample closet and storage space, fold-down desk that doubles as a table, and a bench seat in back that folds down to a queen-size bed. Small windows set into the trolley-top roof and large windows that disappear into the walls provide light and ventilation.

While not exactly designed for comfort, the front seat accommodates two cozy campers. Everything is original, including the honey-toned oak trim and what appears to be the world's largest rearview mirror.

THE ROAD YACHT

FOR FAMILY WEEKENDS • VACATIONS • SEMI-PERMANENT LIVING

The "road yacht" touring car with living accommodations for five persons. Below: luncheon from the "galley" is spread for the auto's driver

The vehicle, which looks like a large metal bug on wheels, is the latest in touring luxury. Speed of forty-five miles an hour may be easily attained. An electric "galley," completely fitted lavatory, two sleeping cabins, book shelves, writing tables, and a radio complete the equipment of this automotive innovation, which accommodates five persons.

"Road Yacht"

$985

A Complete Home

Note compactness of bathroom unit which combines tub and shower, lavatory and roomy towel cabinet

SEE & BUY AT THE 1928 AUTO SHOWS • DEALERSHIPS ARE OPEN

It's not clear if the 1928 Road Yacht ever went into production or where it was made. The right-hand drive indicates that it was produced in the United Kingdom, but the price in dollars suggests that it may have been intended for export to the United States. What is clear is that the streamlined design was very advanced for the time, no doubt contributing to its ability to achieve a blistering speed of 45 miles per hour. The Road Yacht's cabin sports a luxurious bathroom, cooking accommodations, and two sleeping areas. Courtesy Art Himsl collection.

The Thompson Raise the Roof Four-Sleeper and Diner Cabin Sedan looks like a cross between an armored car and limousine. Walter J. Thompson, an inventor and watchmaker who resided in Ontario, California, created the vehicle. From the mid-1920s to the early '30s, Thompson fabricated four boxy house cars, each of which were mounted on flatbed truck chassis. At the same time he was building his squarish house cars, he was also designing this streamlined house car. In 1934, after six years of planning and one year of tinkering, his one-of-a-kind creation was finally roadworthy.

The chassis of the house car is a 1933 Studebaker with an 11 foot 6 inch wheelbase. Interior features include a stove, refrigerator, sink, and sleeping accommodations for four. Without a doubt the most interesting feature of the Thompson house car is the patented telescoping roof that raises by an ingenious series of gears. The Thompson was featured in the November 27, 1937, issue of the British magazine Motor, in which it was described as a "caravan car." It then made an appearance in the December 13, 1937, issue of Life magazine. The Thompson is one of the shining gems in the Vince Martinico Auburn Trailer Collection.

When the roof is fully extended, folks can stand upright in the Thompson. With the steering wheel folded forward, the seats lay back so four can sleep comfortably. A refrigerator, stove, and sink with running water are in the galley at the rear.

It's hard to believe that this stylish motorhome was built in 1937. Dubbed the Zeppelin by its current owner, famed customizer Art Himsl, the Zeppelin started out its life as a prototype house car built by a mechanic at the Chris-Craft boat dealership in San Francisco. A San Francisco doctor who had high hopes of manufacturing a number of them commissioned the vehicle, but World War II material shortages effectively ended his quest. Although this is certainly a unique vehicle, records show that it was registered in 1942 as a Plymouth house car.

Himsl discovered the vehicle in 1968 when he and his friend Ed Green saw the aft end of it sticking out of a barn in California's Napa Valley. Himsl and Green used the vehicle for a few years as sort of an office, but they did not begin a serious restoration until 1999. The first order of business was to refurbish and modernize the drive components. Air-lift bags were added to all four corners, a 350 Chevy engine replaced the old flathead engine, and most of the old running gear was replaced. The original skin on the vehicle was a mixture of steel panels and stretched fabric. Himsl ripped off all the old skin and replaced it with a modern material called Stitz Poly-Fiber. Fenders were replaced (the original vehicle did not have front fenders), the nose was reconstructed, and Himsl applied a spectacular finish in an Art Deco theme. The vehicle was rechristened in 2002 as the 1937 Himsl Zeppelin Roadliner. Photographed in Concord, California.

As part of the restoration of the Roadliner, the original exterior panels were stripped away, which revealed the ribs of the frame. Courtesy Art Himsl.

Upholsterer/designer Howdy Ledbetter executed the inside refurbishment of the Zeppelin's upholstery. He worked around the original oak cabinetry, which had been adapted to house a microwave, refrigerator, magazine rack, and kitchen table that adapts into an additional bed. Ledbetter made dozens of light cream vinyl panels that cover all of the interior; stretched a vinyl covering, which came out of a '78 Cadillac, over the seats; and covered the floors in maroon carpet.

This futuristic-looking streamlined house car was designed by noted industrial designer Brooks Stevens. In 1938, Stevens, who had offices in Milwaukee, was commissioned by the Racine, Wisconsin, firm S. C. Johnson and Son (maker of Johnson's Wax) to build a combination camp and house car, mobile laboratory, and an emergency medical service vehicle. It was proposed that the vehicle be transported to Brazil where it would be used to field test the wax derived from Carnauba palm trees. The Johnson company was well aware of the publicity such a vehicle would bring and made sure it was painted the company color, Cherokee red, and finished off with Johnson Wax-O-Namel.

The 23-foot-long front-wheel-drive house car was built by Linn Corporation of Oneonta, New York. When completed, the vehicle took a short maiden voyage around New York State and then went to the 1939 New York World's Fair. Eventually the vehicle made it to Brazil. In the 1940s, it was the subject of numerous magazine and newspaper articles since it attracted attention wherever it went. When acquired by Vince Martinico, the Brooks Stevens was in sad repair. Much of the credit for the house car's restoration goes to master metal-fabricator Jim Gracier.

The interior of the Brooks Stevens house car is currently undergoing restoration. The original vehicle has, thanks to the front wheel drive, over six feet of standing room. It is equipped with single beds, a convertible sofa bed, stove, refrigerator, sink, table, and a full bathroom with shower. The Brooks Stevens is owned by Vince Martinico/ Auburn Trailer Collection. Photographed in Auburn, California.

Motion picture cameraman John Roy Hunt had a long career in the film business that started in 1904 at the St. Louis World's Fair where he was a film operator. He opened a theater in Fresno, California, in 1905 and then worked as a cameraman. Some of the feature films he photographed were A Daughter of the Gods (1916), Beau Geste (1926), and I Walked with a Zombie (1943). His last film was The Juggler (1953) with Kirk Douglas. A consummate tinkerer (he invented several camera improvements and was a ham radio operator), Hunt built this vehicle in the late 1940s with the hope of manufacturing many more. That dream never came to pass, but many of his innovations were later incorporated by other manufacturers when motorhomes emerged from one-of-a-kind vehicles to mainstream transportation. The main deficiency of the Hunt Hollywood house car was its woefully inadequate power plant, a 1939 Mercury V8 95-horsepower engine (modern motorhomes have at least 300 horsepower). Those 95 ponies were hard pressed to push the 18-foot, 2½-ton house car up any significant grade. A major restoration of the exterior skin of the Hunt was undertaken in 2005 by Monty Osborn, who spent over three hundred hours sanding and polishing the Hunt to achieve a lustrous shine. Photographed by the American River, Coloma, California. Courtesy Vince Martinico collection.

Nowadays people complain about drivers motoring down the road while talking on cell phones. Imagine seeing someone making coffee, frying eggs, or doing the dishes while driving. All of these things were possible in the Hunt although they may have been a bit hazardous to the driver as well as the other vehicles on the road.

Despite its modest size, the Hunt had ample room for seating and sleeping. Every square inch of space was used and items did double duty, including the seats that converted into beds. The entire interior was paneled in birch plywood, that was stained, and varnished to achieve a golden glow.

In 1935, Austrian-born designer Alexius Pribil designed a teardrop-shaped house car while he was president of the Saginaw Stamping and Tool Company in Saginaw, Michigan. A prototype of the vehicle, dubbed the Aircar, was constructed in early 1937 with the assistance of racecar driver Ray Harroun, also an employee of the company. In September 1937, the editors of Modern Mechanix featured the Aircar, now christened the Trailmobile, on the cover, albeit with some artistic license. The article's author speculated that house cars like the Trailmobile could soon replace travel trailers since the tidy rolling homes eliminated problems associated with trailers, such as the maintenance of extra axles and tires, faulty hitches, and poor acceleration capacity. Other problems included poor rear visibility, which made parking difficult. The author went on to suggest that some of the advantages of this self-propelled unit were that the heat from the exhaust pipes could be used for cooking and that a home crafts-man could convert a touring car into a Trailmobile-like vehicle for a few hundred dollars, far less than the cost of buying a trailer. Around the same time the article appeared in Modern Mechanix, Pribil, with a desire to formally manufacture his invention, founded the Pribil Safety Aircar Company, but his death in 1938 put an end to his plan. Courtesy Ray Bystrom collection.

In 1940, movie-mogul Howard Hughes commissioned eight mobile dressing rooms for his company, RKO Studios (now Paramount). This 19-foot vehicle, with 15 feet of usable interior space, is built on a heavy-duty GMC chassis that was originally designed for military vehicles. Indeed, its instrument panel has a decidedly industrial look to it. The driver's and passenger's seats are the same as those used in the Ford Tri-Motor airplane, and the headlights are equipped with side blackout lights. The vehicle is also equipped with a generator, which provided power when the vehicle was used in remote mountain and desert locations.

One of the vehicles first assignments was as a dressing room for Jane Russell during filming of the controversial movie The Outlaw. Much of the controversy revolved around Russell's attributes, cleverly referred to in one advertisement for the film: "What are the two reasons for Jane Russell's rise to stardom?"

The vehicle was sold to a collector during the RKO liquidation auction in 1958 for the then staggering sum of $12,000, but it wound up moldering away in eastern Washington. In 2003, it was acquired by John Agnew who is restoring it at Funky Junk Farms in Los Angeles.

The interior of Jane Russell's mobile dressing room is equipped with some rather advanced features for 1940, including an electric refrigerator, a stove and oven, and a full bathroom with toilet and shower. The entire ensemble is sheathed in beautifully finished mahogany paneling.

THE PICTURE THAT COULDN'T BE STOPPED!

Howard Hughes' GREAT NEW PICTURE

THE OUTLAW

In Person!

JANE RUSSELL

1943'S MOST *exciting* NEW SCREEN STAR

The Outlaw's release was delayed for some time as the Motion Picture Production Code Board (commonly called Hayes Code) pondered the turpitude of some of the scenes. Chief among their tasks was the consideration of Russell's endowments that, thanks to some cleverly engineered foundation garments, got more attention than the other stars in the film. The Outlaw was finally released in 1943 (general release in 1946) to less-than-enthusiastic reviews. But those reviews hardly mattered to producer Howard Hughes. The public's appetite was already whetted, and the box office returns more than made up for all the costs of the legal machinations.

The woody is a truly an iconic American vehicle. This predecessor of today's SUV conjures up images of fun and recreation, especially when a couple of surfboards are strapped on top. But the woody's roots are more utilitarian, as the first production models that appeared in the 1930s were service vehicles that had wood bodies mounted on truck frames. Many of them were used by resorts to transport guests and their luggage back and forth between the resort and the train station. Hence the name station wagon.

The real boom in woodies happened immediately after World War II when raw materials to manufacture motor vehicles were in short supply—that is, most materials except wood. Motor vehicle manufacturers were also required by the government to keep the prices of vehicles at their prewar levels, unless they had a new body. Thus the woody body style was adopted by the big three automakers, General Motors, Ford, and Chrysler, so they could sell them at whatever price the market would bear. These versatile vehicles found a ready market among the newly minted postwar families. In addition to transporting the children and groceries, they became a recreation and camping vehicle, much like the auto camps of the early twentieth century. As raw materials became more readily available, auto manufacturers switched to steel bodies and the resale value of woodies plummeted. Because of their low prices and their ability to hold lots of cargo, they became the vehicle of choice for the beach crowd. Nowadays, expertly restored woodies can command prices well over $100,000. Brad Boyajian owns this award-winning 1946 Chrysler Town and Country convertible woody. Photographed in Chatsworth, California.

In the wake of World War II, automobile manufacturers scrambled to make vehicles that could be used for recreation and camping. The 1951 Kaiser featured a double-hinged articulated trunk and fold-down seats that allowed for sleeping and hauling. "It provides carrying space for anything from minnow net to a moose," claimed an advertisement. Courtesy Vince Martinico collection.

CAMPERS AND VANS

Slide-in campers and retrofitted vans are models of compact convenience. The bits and pieces necessary for creating a home on wheels are pared down to the basics. The first mass-produced slide-in campers were created in the aftermath of World War II when sportsmen and new families with limited budgets looked for ways to have outdoor vacations and adventures without having to stay in flimsy tents or pay for motels and hotels. The tidy size of the campers also allowed more adventurous souls to negotiate back roads where larger vehicles and trailers feared to tread.

The first truck campers were little more than plywood and aluminum boxes set into a pickup truck's bed, but eventually manufacturers started offering bigger units with a sleeping area cantilevered over the cab of the truck and a lilliputian bathroom shoehorned into a space overhanging the back of the truck. Slide-in truck campers have the distinct advantage of having a take-it-along or leave-it-at-home option. Their main disadvantage is that the cab area and the camper area are two discrete areas, a problem that is ably addressed by the camper van, which though nondetachable allows egress between the driver's area and the living area. Camper vans aren't much different from house cars and camp cars; it is not much of a stretch to say that camper vans are essentially modern-day versions of those early-day RVs.

Pickup trucks have always provided a ready receptacle for campers. Their compact size and rugged construction make them ideal foundations to built a tidy camper suited for a weekend outing or an extended stay. When John and Dot Flis decided to get a camper in the mid-1990s, they didn't want any of the pedestrian-looking offerings at the RV dealerships. They wanted something unique and fun that suited their personalities and lifestyle. That sort of wish list, whether in a home or RV, is usually best fulfilled by designing it yourself and that's precisely what John and Dot did. The couple are avid antiquers and in particular they like to go to farm shows and tractor rallies, often with a trailer in tow just in case they find something to their liking. Their love of all things old led them to a 1940 International pickup, which they found moored behind a barn in southern Michigan. After purchasing the truck, the division of labor was established with John assigned to work on the mechanics and Dot appointed to work on the nest.

The result is affectionately called the Shack. John replaced the old engine with a robust 350 Chevy engine and beefed up the suspension and drive train to enable the truck to support the camper and tow a trailer while, according to John, "driving down the highway with the big boys." Dot turned her thoughts to the camper and designed a wheeled farmhouse with a galvanized roof, plywood siding, birdhouse, flowerpot, and taillights made from kerosene lanterns. Photographed in Camp Dearborn, Michigan.

The interior of the Shack has all the comforts of home (albeit on a reduced scale), including a sink, small refrigerator that runs on propane or electricity, microwave, porta-potty, wall-to-wall carpet, vaulted ceiling, and air conditioning. "It even has a washer and dryer," says John, who illustrates his claim by holding up a coat hanger with a large steel washer dangling at the center.

The CREE Pick-Up Truck COACH

Three LUXURIOUS MODELS fit all makes of PICK-UP TRUCKS

Two pickup campers emerged almost simultaneously in the mid-1940s—the Cree camper in the Midwest and the Sport King on the West Coast. The Cree Truck Coach was manufactured in Marcellus, Michigan, by Howard Cree. Cree had operated a travel trailer and cabin campground, Cree's Log Cabin and Trailer Court, and had a trailer dealership near Detroit. In the latter stages of World War II, Cree sold his business and purchased a Ford dealership in Marcellus. Capitalizing on the burgeoning vacation market that emerged after World War II and drawing inspiration from some of the homemade campers he had seen at his trailer court, Cree came up with an idea for combining a trailer and a pickup truck. The result of his tinkering was a boxy little camper that he dubbed the Cree Pick-Up Truck Coach. The first models were displayed at a sports-and-travel show at Navy Pier in Chicago in 1945 and shortly thereafter orders came pouring in.

Cree Coaches were offered in 8- and 10-foot models and were also available mounted on a chassis so they could be converted into a trailer and pulled by an automobile. The Cree Coaches were homely and utilitarian, to be sure, but they marked an important milestone in RV history. Unlike trailers, they were much easier to maneuver and unlike house cars, the camper could be left behind when not needed. Courtesy Milton Newman collection.

Walter King is known as the father of the pickup camper. He helped popularize pickup campers with the innovations he developed. Chief among them were the first cabover camper and the first large-scale production line for campers. King, who grew up in Boys Town, Nebraska, journeyed to California in the late 1930s as a young man. It was there that he developed his love of the outdoors. While in California, he designed and built a teardrop trailer. In the fall of 1944, he and a couple of buddies hitched up the tiny trailer to a pickup truck and took off on a hunting expedition to Montana. The trio soon found that cooking outside the trailer and trying to fit three bodies inside during inclement weather was more than a little challenging. At one point, King wondered why they weren't using the truck as part of their camping accommodations. When King returned to California, he began sketching ideas for a camper that would nestle into a pickup truck's bed. Materials were in short supply in the latter years of World War II, but when the war ended in August 1945, King, aided by a finely tuned set of plans he had been working on, was ready to build his camper.

As materials became available in the first weeks after the war ended, King devoted all the time he could to building his homemade truck camper so it would be ready for hunting season that fall. He completed the camper in time. On this hunting trip, King brought along his wife instead of his two buddies. He and his wife could now sleep and cook in comfort, freed from the confines of the teardrop trailer. At one point, the couple encountered a crusty old sheepherder who enquired about their tidy little camper. A conversation and negotiations ensued and soon King found himself in possession of five $100 bills that the sheepherder gave him as a deposit for five campers King agreed to make as soon as he returned to California.

After returning to California, King hastily set up a modest production line in Torrance, and commenced to build the campers. A few months later, the sheepherder and four of his friends showed up at King's factory with their pickup trucks and took delivery of their campers. Within a few months, orders started coming in from Montana and Idaho, obviously from people who had seen King's campers. Sensing that things were going well, King attended a sports-and-hobby show in Long Beach, California, and exhibited his camper. The only other recreational vehicles at the show were a smattering of travel trailers, so King's creation got a lot of attention. During the show, one of the attendees suggested that King could improve his product by utilizing the unused space over the cab and commissioned King to build what would be the first cabover camper.

King expanded his product line in the early 1950s by offering small travel trailers and in the 1970s by offering motorhomes. The company officially closed its doors in 1987.

Pictured is a 1949 Sport King camper on a 1952 Ford F2 truck. Promoted as "the World's Greatest Trucks," the F-Series Ford was an able platform for a pickup camper because of its long-standing reputation of durability and reliability. The duo is owned by Milton Newman. Photographed at the Travnikar Compound, Penryn, California.

Early Sport Kings were available in 8-, 9-, and 10-foot models with four floor plans available for each model. Seen here is an 8-foot model, with a dinette floor plan, that sold for approximately $845. The Sport King's owner has gone to great lengths to keep the interior authentic to the era. Interior embellishments include a copy of Outdoor Life magazine, a vintage 35-millimeter camera, hand-pump Black Flag bug sprayer, and a Hiawatha water jug. Of particular note is the late 1940s vintage linoleum with a cowboys-and-Indians motif, a real treasure for collectors.

Without a doubt, one of the most interesting camper innovations was the hydraulically assisted pop-up camper. The camper was the invention of R. D. Hall. Hall grew up in Rochester, New York, attended the Rochester Institute of Technology, and then served in World War II. After the war, he settled in California but yearned to explore Alaska. He knew that accommodations in Alaska were few and far between and the trip to Alaska on the Alcan Highway presented its own set of challenges. Mindful of the challenges that laid ahead, Hall designed and built a camper for the three-month trip.

Hall's design attracted so much attention and acclaim that he started formally building the campers under the Alaskan Campers name in 1958. By 1962, there were five factories in the United States and two in Canada manufacturing the campers. The major element that separated the Alaskan from other campers was the telescoping roof that was operated with a hydraulic assist. The clever idea of having a telescoping top, which has since been widely imitated, allows for generous headroom when camping and provides a more ground-hugging streamlined profile while in motion.

In its advertising, Alaskan capitalized on the advantages of having a camper instead of a trailer: "No license is required for the Alaskan Camper. It is lawful to carry passengers enroute. Passengers may rest or sleep in ample comfort, play cards, etc., while the miles go skimming by." The advertising, however, does not mention how those activities are comfortably accomplished with the top in the retracted position.

Alaskan Campers are still being manufactured and continue to be regarded as one of the most durable and highest-quality campers on the market. They are available in 8- and 10-foot lengths. The 1967 8-foot Alaskan Camper and 1968 Chevrolet truck with a Serves utility body are owned by Milton Newman. Photographed at the Travnikar Dandelion Sanctuary, Penryn, California.

The interior view of the Alaskan Camper illustrates the ample 6 feet 4 inches of headroom available when the top is raised. The 8- and 10-foot models had identical accessories, but the 10-foot boasted a bigger dinette and sleeping area. Accouterments included a three-burner propane stove, ice box, and pump-operated faucet with storage tank. Available options were a propane-powered refrigerator, propane furnace for those frigid Alaskan winters, and a stovetop oven.

What could be more all-American than the Nelson family? The Adventures of Ozzie and Harriet, which ran on ABC television from 1952–66, tracked the day-to-day lives of the Nelson family and, in particular, the youngest son, Ricky, who grew to be a bona fide teenage heartthrob. In this promotional photograph, Ozzie Nelson emerges from an Alaskan Camper while Ricky (on the left) and David stand outside. Harriet is, no doubt, preparing a fine family meal in the camper's tidy galley. Courtesy Alaskan Campers.

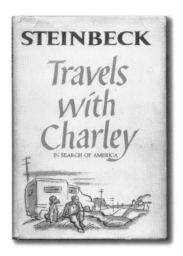

Before Steinbeck embarked on his journey, many of his neighbors came by his home in Sag Harbor, New York, to inspect his future home on wheels. Steinbeck wrote, "I saw in their eyes something I was to see over and over in every part of the nation—a burning desire to go, to move, to get underway, anyplace, away from any Here. They spoke quietly of how they wanted to go someday, to move about, free and unanchored."

This early brochure, from 1961, depicts the pleasures to be had in the great outdoors and while merrily rolling down the road in an Alaskan Camper. Courtesy Milton Newman collection.

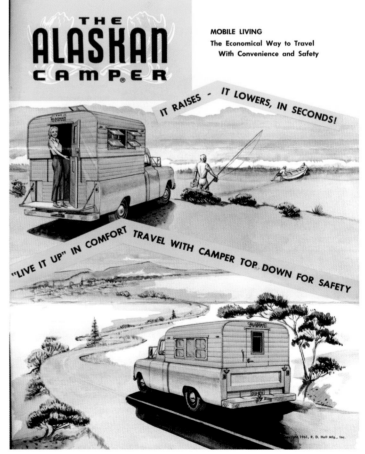

" A journey is a person in itself; no two are alike. **"** **"** We find **after years** of struggle **that we do not take a trip; a trip takes us. "**

(*Travels with Charley*)

There are few RV adventures as well documented as John Steinbeck's were in his 1961 novel, Travels with Charley. On September 23, 1960, Steinbeck along with his aged poodle Charley hopped into his brand new 1961 GMC pickup truck saddled with a Wolverine camper and took off on a ten-thousand-mile, two-month odyssey in search of America. Steinbeck had suffered a small stroke in December 1959 and his wife and friends had expressed concern about his undertaking such an arduous journey, but it was something he felt compelled to do. Much of his trip had to do with seeing America from a down-to-earth perspective and re-experiencing the lives of the migrant farm workers he had documented so well in his book The Grapes of Wrath, which was set during the Great Depression.

True to the form of many RVers, Steinbeck felt compelled to name his rig. After a bit of pondering, he decided to christen it Rocinante after Don Quixote's horse because many of Steinbeck's friends felt that the trip was quixotic. Travels with Charley was the icing on the cake of Steinbeck's career. He won the Nobel Prize for literature in 1962 "for his realistic and imaginative writings, combining as they do sympathetic humour and keen social perception." John Steinbeck died on December 20, 1968. On April 1, 1998, Rocinante was moved into its permanent home in the main exhibit gallery of the National Steinbeck Center in Salinas, California.

The camper, which was manufactured by the Wolverine Camper Company in Glaswin, Michigan, had the feel of a cozy cabin, thanks to its honey-toned wood interior. Although somewhat spartan by today's standards, the Wolverine was equipped with the basic necessities of a stove, refrigerator, chemical toilet, bed, and table. Amongst the beverages on the table is a bottle of Courvoisier Cognac, a libation that Steinbeck had a predilection for and celebrated in a number of his writings. The typewriter, while not the one that was used to write his travel journals, is similar to the real one, a Swiss-made Hermes Baby that resides at the Center for Steinbeck Studies at San Jose State University.

The Avion and Cayo campers were an outgrowth of the trailers manufactured by the Avion Coach Corporation of Benton Harbor, Michigan. Avion, which was founded in 1955 by Allen Grams, Loren Cayo, and Larry Zuhl, was originally named Romany Coach, Inc., but the name was changed to Avion when Romany Gypsies objected to their name being used on a decidedly un-Romany trailer. The most distinctive feature of the Avion trailer is the all-aluminum exterior, which to the casual eye makes it look very much like an Airstream trailer. The trailer company prospered in the 1950s, and in the early '60s the owners looked to the rapidly expanding slide-in camper market as a way to increase their product offerings.

The Avion and Cayo campers were essentially the same camper. Cayo replaced the Avion name in July 1970 when Robert Cayo acquired the pickup-camper division of Avion. Avions and Cayos were sheathed in the same anodized aluminum as the Avion trailers, which eliminated the need for polishing. They utilized riveted construction, which was touted as being rattle proof. The first campers rolled off the production line in 1965, and production continued until the early 1970s. The campers originally came in 8½- and 10-foot lengths, with two interior configurations called Deluxe Gaucho Model and Custom Side Dinette. The 10-foot model, the C-10, was the most popular of the two. The now rare 8½-foot model was discontinued after a few years. An 11-foot model, the C-11, was added to the line and continued to be produced along with the C-10. The Avion legacy lives on thanks to the Silver Avion Fellowship, which organizes rallies and caravans for members who own aircraft-constructed, riveted Avions and Cayos that were manufactured between 1955 and 1990. The club, which also facilitates communication between members, can be reached at silveravion@frontier.net.

The six Avion and Cayo campers pictured above are (left to right) a 1966 Avion owned by Terry Prentkowski and Bernie Stuckey, 1969 Avion C-11 owned by Brian and Joyce Smithson, 1967 Avion C-11 owned by Dick and Peg Hale, 1965 Avion C-10 owned by Art Dietrich and Heidi Hough, 1966 Avion C-10 owned by Bill and Denise Fletcher, and 1971 Cayo owned by Ralph Burcar. Photographed in Camp Dearborn, Michigan.

This 1965 10-foot Avion C-10 was, according to the owners, the thirtieth camper built by Avion. The truck is a 1975 Ford Camper Special. Owned by Heidi Hough and Art Detrich. Photographed in Camp Dearborn, Michigan.

The interior of this 1971 10-foot Cayo camper in a side-dinette configuration features, among other things, a three-burner stove, gas/electric refrigerator, 20-gallon water tank, and a window between the camper and cab of the truck (visible behind the small pillow at the center of the photograph). The camper can sleep four quite cozily: two in the convertible dinette and two in the generously proportioned 50- by 85-inch bed above the cab. Out of view on the right is a bathroom with shower. Ralph Burcar owns the camper. Photographed in Camp Dearborn, Michigan.

Some of the first van conversions were the various incarnations of Metro vans that had previously served as delivery vehicles for many products, including linens, milk, and bread. These tidy little vans (most were around 18 feet long) were readily adapted to homes on wheels, thanks to their sturdy frames and ample headroom. While they hardly rocketed down the highway, they trudged along with a steady-as-she-goes attitude.

This 1951 International Metro Step Van served for a dozen years as a delivery truck for the American Linen Supply Company in St. Paul, Minnesota. It somehow made it to California by way of Las Vegas where its current owners purchased it for a crisp $100 bill in 1969. The little van has been on a number of adventures, including towing a 31-foot Airstream trailer over one hundred thousand miles in four years. During a particularly arduous portion of that journey in Mexico, it acquired its nickname, Tortuga (tortoise). Vern and Kathey Heaney own the Metro van. Photographed at the Deming Log Show Grounds, Bellingham, Washington.

KATHEY & VERN

Shortly after acquiring the van, the owners fitted it with the basics, but it was still little more than a steel tent on wheels.
In the early 1990s, the owners completely redid the interior to prepare for a twelve-thousand-mile, around-the-country
excursion. The interior accoutrements consist of a diminutive stove and icebox, sink, porta-potty, ample storage space in
cabinets and under the bed, and most importantly (according to the owners) a very comfortable full-size bed.

VOLKSWAGEN

It's safe to say that the most well-known and enduring imported vehicle is the humble Volkswagen. The beginnings of the Volkswagen can be traced to arch bad guy Adolf Hitler, who desired an affordable automobile for the German people. One of Hitler's goals for his new society was to build autobahns modeled after wide American roadways. But what good would his autobahns be without vehicles? At the time, the only people who had automobiles were a few wealthy Germans. In 1934, Hitler personally proscribed the design specifications of what would be known as the people's car, the *volks wagen*. Ultimately, the design was turned over to Dr. Ferdinand Porsche, who would go on to design the renowned sports cars that carry his name. The first Porsche-designed Volkswagen rolled off the assembly line on August 15, 1940, and production continued throughout World War II. Most of the units produced during the war were German army vehicles known as Kubelwagens and amphibious vehi-

cles known as Schwimmwagens. Despite the widespread destruction of German industries by the Allies during the war, the Volkswagen factory, located in Wolfburgs, Germany, was up and running by late 1945. In 1947, the first Beetle was offered to the public.

By the late 1940s, Volkswagen designers were looking into the possibility of building a larger van-like vehicle. The van's original design is credited to Ben Pod, a Volkswagen importer from the Netherlands who sketched his design on a cocktail napkin in 1947. By 1949, eight bus prototypes known as Transporters, or Bullis, were tested, all powered by a modest 25-horsepower engine. Six of these of these were dubbed Panelvans, another was called a Kombi, and the last was named a Microbus. The Transporters were an instant success. By 1951, the first Microbus Deluxe, also known as the Samba, was introduced and a few pickup trucks and ambulances were even produced. In the first few years of

Two 1969 Volkswagen Westfalias exhibit their pop-up sleeping compartments. John and Mary Jane Merschdorf own the pearl white van. Chuck and Donna Simpson own the red van. Both were photographed in Camp Dearborn, Michigan.

Volkswagen owners are a dedicated breed, often nurturing their aging vans far beyond their projected life. Such is the case with this orange 1973 Kombi with a quarter million miles, many of them logged on dusty back roads of Utah and Nevada. Miraculously the paint is original, and the only maintenance to its lustrous finish is an occasional waxing and buffing. The Kombi was retrofitted with the Campmobile package, which includes a sink, dining table, bench seat that converts into a bed, louvered side windows with curtains, child's cot that fits across the flight deck, closet, storage cabinets, and rear bug screen. Volkswagens have a habit of appearing in motion pictures, most notably in Disney's Herbie films. This orange Kombi had a cameo role in another Disney film, Meet the Deedles. The van is owned by Salt Lake City-based author/photographer Richard Menzies. Photographed at the Scott Shady Court, Winnemucca, Nevada.

production, dozens of different configurations were applied to the Transporters, including fire trucks, office vans, cleaning vans, mobile butcher shops, refrigerated ice cream vans, and beer wagons. Almost as soon as the first Transporters rolled off the assembly line, people started turning them into camping vehicles. Volkswagen took note of this phenomenon and set its engineers to work on a dedicated camping vehicle.

Although Volkswagen wound up producing a camper, it turned over the manufacture of a higher-end camping vehicle to a coach-building company in Wiedenbrück, Germany, in the Westfalia region. In 1951, the Westfalia Camper was born. A number of configurations of the Volkswagen Campers and Westfalia Campers were built throughout the 1950s, '60s, and '70s.

The 1960s were the heyday of the Volkswagen. Volkswagens were the vehicle of choice for the emerging eco-conscious crowd, young hipsters, and folks who just wanted to be a little different. The most popular model was the Bug, but there were also vans, campers, and even trucks.

The owner of the pictured vehicle wanted a camper, so after consulting with Perris Valley Campers of Perris Valley, California, he did the necessary prep work on the 1966 VW truck, which included removing the tailgate and luggage doors and cutting out a section of the bed. The stripped-down VW truck was left at Perris Valley and the work was done (appropriately) by a guy named Mac. Perris Valley Campers went out of business in 1989. The camper eventually made it to Michigan where it was purchased by its current owner, Michael Jernigan. Photographed on the grounds of the Sloane Museum, Flint, Michigan.

They became the hippie van of choice for the flower power generation. In 1979, the Vanagon was rolled out, and over the years it has been available in a number of different models, including the multi-van Magnum; White Star; Blue Star; European Westfalia Camper; Joker, renamed California; a rare limited edition of the Westfalia Camper, the Wolfsburg edition called the Atlantic; Carat; Multi-van; Weekender; and full Westfalia camper models called Vanagon GL Camper and Vanagon GL Westfalia Camper.

ULTRA VAN

The history of the Ultra Van can be traced to California RVer Dave Peterson. Peterson, who worked as an aircraft designer at Boeing and Beech, had a Spartan trailer and also a boat. When he went on outdoor adventures, he had to choose between the comfort of the living space of the trailer and the recreational aspect of the boat, a dilemma that caused him to ponder ways to build a motorized trailer so he could tug his boat along behind it. The answer came in 1959 when General Motors introduced the 80-horsepower, 140-cubic-inch rear-engine-powered Corvair, an automobile that would later achieve a measure of fame as the subject of Ralph Nader's 1965 book *Unsafe at Any Speed*. Employing his aircraft-design knowledge, Peterson used the monocoque construction techniques of the aircraft industry to construct a body that needed neither frame nor chassis. The front and rear sections were made of fiberglass while the center section was made of an aluminum skin stretched over aluminum ribs. The low-slung design afforded a pleasing profile, plenty of interior space in its modestly proportioned 22- x 8- x 8-foot body and helped the Ultra Van attain a respectable 15 to 17 miles per gallon. Prior to this, monocoque construction techniques were used in trailers as early as the mid-1930s when sailplane-pioneer Hawley Bowlus built his Bowlus-Teller trailers, but the techniques had never been used in any production motor coaches.

After renting a warehouse space in the fall of 1960, Peterson hired students from a local technical school. Four months later, the first unit, christened the Go-Home, poked its nose out the door. In all, Peterson and his students produced about fifteen Go-Homes, which sold for around $7,000. In 1963, the Prescolite Corporation, a manufacturer of light fixtures ordered some of the units (now dubbed

Forrest Gist owns this 1968 Ultra Van #413. Photographed at the Deming Log Show Grounds, Bellingham, Washington.

Barbara and Paul Piché of Berkley, Michigan, acquired this happy 1968 Ultra Van #389 in 1996. They are long-time members of the Tin Can Tourists and the Ultra Van clubs, and their van often serves as a commuter vehicle, transporting rally attendees from location to location. When traveling down the road, their friendly whale-like van always elicits smiles. Photographed in Camp Dearborn, Michigan.

Travalons) to be used as mobile showrooms. By 1964, Peterson's creation had attracted the attention of John Tillotson, a publisher in Kansas. Tillotson negotiated a license from Peterson and opened up shop in an unused aircraft hanger at an old Naval Base in Hutchinson, Kansas. He renamed the unit the Ultra Van.

The area around Hutchinson was home to many people who were trained in aircraft construction in World War II and was also close to Wichita, home of the Cessna Aircraft Corporation. Thus, craftsmen and managers, already familiar with monocoque fabrication techniques were the first employees of Ultra, Inc. By the end of 1966, eight Ultra Vans a month, with a price tag of $8,995, were gliding off the assembly line.

Ultra Vans never had staggering sales (less than four hundred in various configurations were built). Rumors, which eventually proved true, that Corvair would cease production, a price in 1968 that hovered around $10,000, and competition

from other manufacturers spelled the end for the Ultra Van; the plant was closed in June 1970. In 1972 and 1973, founder Dave Peterson, attempting to revive the company, built five slightly longer units powered by an Oldsmobile Rocket V8 engine, but the 1973 energy crisis and subsequent gas shortages were too much for the tiny company to weather, and Peterson had to close up shop for good.

Thanks to the rustproof aluminum and fiberglass construction, many of the Ultra Vans are still on the road. In fact, the Ultra Van Motor Coach Club (UVMCC) can account for close to 250 of the 373 or so Ultra Vans believed to have been manufactured. This is a surprisingly high number considering the last production model came off the assembly line in 1970. Ultra Van owners hold rallies, at which they proudly display their Ultra Van number, from time to time just like Airstream owners. The original prototype, #101, was found in 1991 and was restored by club members. It is now on display in a museum in Tennessee.

All Ultra Vans have the same basic interior configuration, and they usually have an array of special custom features installed by each owner. A large bed is mounted in the aft section directly over the engine. Depending on the age and repair of the drive-train and insulation, the engine can provide warmth at night. On the right side of the interior are a small bathroom, stove, refrigerator, and sink. A couch that converts into additional sleeping space hugs the left side, and two ample seats on swivels complete the interior. Ultra Van owners are particularly fond of the huge wrap-around windshield and other large windows that make the interior seem much larger. Norm and Marion Helmkay own this Ultra Van #408. Photographed in Camp Dearborn, Michigan.

This smiling Ultra Van #408 is one of four restored by the Helmkays. A plaque on the front that reads "831" refers to the van's FMCA (Family Motor Coach Association) number. Photographed in Camp Dearborn, Michigan.

Vixens, which were produced from 1986 to 1989, are a fabulous example of how having a good idea, innovativeness, sound engineering, and quality components doesn't necessarily guarantee success. The Vixen was the brainchild of William T. Collins, a former executive of Pontiac and the ill-fated DeLorean Motor Company. Collins believed there was a market for a sleek, stylish motorhome that was stingy on fuel. That market, Collins said, was young urban professionals, better known as Yuppies. Collins fashioned an easy-to-drive, aerodynamic motorhome that was easy on fuel and according to its advertising, "Goes through the wind like a knife through water." Any Yuppie would be proud to park it next to his BMW in his three-car suburban garage, thought Collins. As a matter of fact, he reasoned, why not sell it through car dealerships rather than RV dealerships? Yuppies need not rub elbows with the geriatric crowd. Collins proclaimed that the Vixen wouldn't be introduced at the big RV shows; instead, its debut would be at the elegant Detroit Auto Show. With his game plan in place, Collins started producing the innovative and trendy Vixens.

To be sure, the Vixen sported a number of innovations. First and foremost was a BMW turbo-diesel power plant that delivered close to 30 miles per gallon. Inside accoutrements included a full-size, permanently-made-up double bed in the rear, a shower that had its water heated via a heat exchanger hooked up to the engine, an additional diesel water heater and furnace, 12- and 115-volt electrical system, and an air-suspension system that provided a smooth ride and doubled as levelers when in a campground. Best of all, and unique to the Vixen, was the roof that could be raised to provide over 6 feet 6 inches of interior space. When lowered, however, the exterior of the vehicle was only 6 feet 4 inches tall and could be tucked into a regular garage.

From 1986 to 1989, 587 Vixens were produced in the Pontiac, Michigan, facility. Three hundred and seventy-six were turbo diesels, thirty-nine were limousines, and the remainder were gasoline powered. Their steep price tag, which ranged from $40,000 to $53,000, may have been somewhat of a deterrent, but the real mistake was that Collins didn't do his homework. If he had, he would have discovered that Yuppies simply did not buy motorhomes and that motorhomes should be sold through a motorhome dealer. Ken Mantz owns this 1987 Vixen. Photographed in Hutchinson, Kansas.

Camper rentals are very popular in Australia and represent a way for tourists to get a more authentic Australian experience. Wicked Campers rents a variety of campervans from the austere (no air conditioning) to the deluxe (air conditioning and power steering). All of the campers are brightly painted, often with scenes from Australia. This platypus-themed, converted Mazda van is painted in the Australian aboriginal dot painting style that originated over fifty thousand years ago in central Australia. Aborigines didn't have a written language, so dot paintings were a way of telling a short story. Photographed in the parking lot of the Giant Earthworm Museum, Gippsland, Australia.

BUS CONVERSIONS

Long before recreational vehicle manufacturers were churning out motorhomes on assembly lines, private individuals and a smattering of small firms were turning buses into motorized living quarters. Many of the first bus conversions were built for entertainers who spent a lot of time on the road and needed a vehicle to transport their equipment and also serve as temporary sleeping quarters when hotel accommodations could not be found or were simply too expensive. Buses make an ideal foundation for a motorhome since they already have a substantial frame and power plant. Another advantage of bus conversions is that they allow one to build a motorhome at an entry-level price. If the bus is in sound mechanical condition, mechanically apt owners can do much of the work themselves.

Bus conversions achieved their greatest notoriety in the 1960s and '70s when members of the flower power generation picked up old buses (church buses seemed to be a favorite) and painted them in sensuous polychrome colors. A number of the color schemes were, without a doubt, inspired by a cornucopia of pharmaceuticals. The most famous bus of this genre was Ken Kesey's bus, Furthur. The misspelling may have simply been an error or the work of Kesey's fun-loving Merry Pranksters. The cross-country journey taken by the bus and its psychedelically fueled passengers is celebrated in Tom Wolfe's award-winning novel *The Electric Kool Aid Acid Test*. In the 1960s, rock-and-roll bands, famous and not yet famous, had their own versions of Kesey's bus. The band The Who had a double-decker bus that graced the cover of their 1968 album, *Magic Bus*. The Beatles made a movie and a landmark album *Magical Mystery Tour* that centered around a Bedford bus. Even television's mainstream Partridge family had a colorful bus, although it was painted in a more ordered color scheme.

Vintage hippie buses are becoming as rare as vintage hippies, so it's unusual to find a bus that is intact as well as operating. This bus started out its life as a dowdy 1964 Chevrolet school bus that was owned by the First Pentecostal Church of Cranston, Rhode Island. Michael Wright acquired it a decade or so later. Michael, who is usually known as Bus Michael because he has owned a number of buses, has, thanks to copious amounts of Bondo and elbow grease, kept the bus in remarkably good repair, long after most hippie buses skidded into the sunset. Thanks to Michael's collection of photographs, the bus's provenance can be accurately plumbed. The bus has made appearances in the Doo Dah Parade (an antidote to the more traditional Rose Parade) in Pasadena, California, which occurs on the weekend before Thanksgiving. Photographed in Slab City, California.

Nowadays, there are hundreds of bus conversions meandering down the nation's roadways. Thanks to their industrial-strength power plants, built for the grueling demands of public transit, bus conversions can have an extended life long after they have been retired from their original duties. There are numerous clubs comprised of devotees of particular brands as well as clubs tailored to bus conversions in general. See the resource section at the end of this book for a listing of bus-conversion clubs and Web sites.

Gypsy caravans and hippie buses are rooted in the same decorative ethos: the joy of excess. Every conceivable surface of this bus's interior is covered with memorabilia. Pictures of friends, found objects, buttons, and beads abound. It seems only fitting that the primary decorative element is pictures of effervescent individuals since most of Michael's buses served as temporary homes for dozens of people. Michael is quick to point out that he alone did not construct the bus and its interior. Many people helped over time. In the aft section of the bus, there is a bed with silent film star Theda Bara hovering above. The popped-up roof provides ample headroom with clerestory windows for ventilation and porthole skylights for additional light. Most of the photographs feature adventures at a variety of hot springs, and most people are depicted au naturel. Notable items in the front of the bus are a wood-burning stove; an overstuffed, tie-dyed hitchhiker's chair on the left; and a couch on the right, which serves as the hitchhiker's bed.

Michael Wright's bus had its most noted exposure as a foil in a photo shoot in 1993 for Mango, a magazine/catalog produced by Barcelona-based fashion designer Mango. Supermodels Claudia Schiffer and Naomi Campbell posed, sulked, and vamped inside and outside the bus in an array of neo-hippie tie-dyed garments. Courtesy Michael Wright collection.

There is no need for a portable DVD player when riding in Michael's bus. Plenty of visuals are supplied to keep you occupied, even on long journeys. Featured prominently is the credo espoused by many flower children, rock-and-roll musicians, and assorted hangers-on: "sex drugz and rock and roll."

Without a doubt, the most famous of the so-called hippie buses was Furthur, a multicolored craft that transported Ken Kesey and his group of friends, known as the Merry Pranksters, on a number of hallucinogenically fueled adventures in the 1960s. In 1964, Kesey, flush with money and fame, thanks to the success of his novel One Flew Over the Cuckoo's Nest, purchased an aged 1939 International school bus with the intent of driving across the country to announce and celebrate the publication of his next book, Sometimes a Great Notion. Kesey enlisted the Merry Pranksters and prepared for the journey. The yellow color of the bus just wouldn't do, so Kesey and the Pranksters applied liberal amounts of swirling polychromatic paint and christened the old bus Furthur, a testament to their continual destination. After stocking the refrigerator with a bottle of orange juice generously laced with LSD-25, an experimental drug at the time, they set off on their own version of the quintessential American road trip.

Kesey and the Pranksters continued to use the bus on a number of adventures, painting it different colors as their mood warranted. Eventually the bus was retired to a pasture on Kesey's farm near Eugene, Oregon, where it reposes today. From time to time, efforts have been made to restore the bus, including a Pranksteresque one by Kesey himself. He created an entirely new bus, using a smaller late '40s-era bus as his canvas. The "new" bus was used for a 1990 re-creation of the Pranksters famous journey. Kesey announced he was going to donate it to the Smithsonian despite the museum's protestations that they only wanted the original bus. After Kesey and the new bus made a number of appearances, the bus was given a coat of dowdy church blue, emblazoned with the words Mt. Pisgah School for the Dumb, and driven off into the sunset. Images of Furthur (now with the correct spelling, Further) courtesy Zane Kesey, www.key-z.com.

A psychedelically painted BMMO (Birmingham and Midland Motor Omnibus Company) double-decker bus graces the cover of this 1968 album, Magic Bus The Who on Tour. The album was never wildly popular with fans of The Who because the hippie theme didn't really go with the band's more earthy identity and, despite the "on tour" designation, the album was simply a compilation of previous songs, none of which were recorded at live concerts.

NOTHING LASTS!

motto of the
Merry Pranksters

FLXIBLE BUS COMPANY

The first bus manufacturer to go into formal production of motorhomes was the Flxible Bus Company of Loudonville, Ohio. The Flxible Bus Company got its start in 1912 as the Flxible Sidecar Company, a manufacturer of motorcycle side-cars. The odd spelling of *Flxible* is derived from the fact that the name *Flexible* couldn't be trademarked. After World War I, demand for motorcycles dropped because of lower auto-mobile prices and safety issues with motorcycles, so Flxible turned its sights to the commercial automobile (ambulances and funeral cars) and bus business. The first Flxible bus rolled off the line in 1924. Throughout the 1930s and '40s, Flxible continued to build buses and other commercial vehicles, most of which were built on a Buick chassis.

Flxible buses, which came in Clipper, VL-100, Hi Level, Flxliner, Starliner, City Bus, and Flxette models, have always ranked high on the list for people who want to turn a bus into a house on wheels. The durability and stylish design of "Flexies" are their chief assets. The most desirable model is the Flxible Clipper, first introduced in the late 1930s, and then widely used by the Greyhound and Trailways bus companies in the 1940s and '50s. Among the luminaries who owned Flxible buses were Buck Owens, Flatt and Scruggs, and Little Richard. Flxible owners like to point to the movie *Key Largo,* starring Humphrey Bogart and Lauren Bacall, in which the first major character was brought into the movie via a Flxible Clipper. The Flxible Company may be no more (in 1996, it filed for bankruptcy and its assets were auctioned), but thanks to a dedicated cadre of Flxible owners it lives on. See the resources section at the end of this book for details on clubs.

The view of the interior towards the aft section illustrates the beautiful, polished mahogany paneling and doors. Rustproof marine-grade hardware is used on the cabinet's hinges and door pulls.

This 1949 Flxible Clipper was originally owned by a man named Fritz, who bought it as a shell in 1950. He installed beautiful mahogany wood cabinets and accents and used long-lasting marine-grade metal for most of the hardware. The current owners, Joe and Gail Pirri, replaced the original Buick Straight Eight engine with a 454 Chevy engine that has an Allison automatic transmission. Photographed at Flywheelers Park, Avon Park, Florida.

This 1941 Flxible Clipper served as an Illinois Transit 24-passenger transit bus in Springfield. Its present owners, Jim and Sheri Reddy, converted it to a motor coach in the late '90s. The chief mechanical change was the replacement of the original Buick Straight Eight engine with a 453 Detroit Diesel engine and the installation of a four-speed transmission. Photographed at the Sloane Museum, Flint, Michigan.

The interior of the 1941 Flxible has all the comforts of a late-twentieth-century home on wheels, including sumptuous captains chairs, microwave, full kitchen, house plants, and that icon of the 1990s—Big Mouth Billy Bass, the animated singing fish.

The 1994 Australian cult film Priscilla Queen of the Desert *may be the only time a motorhome got the title role in a motion picture.* *The movie documents the adventures of three gender-challenged male performers as they make their way across the Australian Outback* *to perform at a nightclub in Alice Springs. Their mode of transportation is an old bus. Along the way, it receives a coat of pink paint. The film* *was so well received by the Aussies that an updated version of Priscilla was commissioned. The new Priscilla, complete with metallic eyelashes,* *supple lips, and a vibrantly coiffed do was fabricated by Stan and Josie Biega from a 1980 Denning Bus and was featured at the closing* *ceremony of the 2000 Olympic Games in Sydney. Alas, Priscilla has been stripped of her accessories and now lives a sedate life as an* *ordinary motorhome. Courtesy Stan and Josie Biega, www.bussalesonline.com.au.*

The Partridge Family, a sitcom that featured a widowed mother and her five children that aired on ABC Television from 1970 until 1974, had its own version of a brightly painted hippie bus. Appropriately the bus was painted in a more geometric (square) pattern than the free-flowing designs of the hippie buses. In the series, the Partridge family acquired a 1957 Chevrolet school bus from Al's Used Cars because they needed a vehicle to transport them and their equipment to a gig at Caesar's Palace in Las Vegas. The family painted the bus in a geometric-style reminiscent of Dutch painter Piet Mondrian, and they were on their way.

After the show's demise, the bus went through a series of owners and eventually wound up lame and abandoned in the parking lot of Lucy's Tacos in East Los Angeles. A short time later, it was junked. When David Cassidy, who played Keith Partridge on the original series, went on a revival tour in 1993, he traveled in a look-alike bus. Another copy of the original bus can be seen at Universal Studios in Florida. For the Partridge-trivia minded, the rear of the bus sported license plate number NLX 590 and a sign that read, "Careful, Nervous Mother Driving."

The Partridge Family series generated a number of spin-off products, including records, refrigerator magnets, lunch boxes, books, posters, and games. In the Partridge Family game, each roll of the dice could put a family on their way to getting on the bus and winning the game or could make the family land on one of the birds and be subject to drawing a card that could put them in peril. For reasons known only to the game's inventor, drawing a Partridge card that says, "LAURIE belongs to the 'now generation,'" causes the player to lose a turn while drawing a card that says, "MOM likes to sing in the shower," advances the player six spaces.

Few American companies have been in business as long as Marmon-Herrington. The company got its start in 1851 as the Nordyke and Marmon Machine Company, a manufacturer of flour mill machinery. The Marmon name became much better known when the company began manufacturing automobiles at the beginning of the twentieth century. The Marmon Wasp won the first Indianapolis 500 race in 1911, and the Marmon Sixteen (a 16-cylinder sedan) was one of the most luxurious automobiles in America. The Great Depression took its toll on the Marmon Car Company. The business decided to employ the services of Arthur Herrington, a retired colonel and military engineer, and concentrate its effort on the manufacture of more utilitarian transports like military vehicles and buses. The company changed its name to Marmon-Herrington. Though still in business, the company no longer manufactures buses. Their main business today is designing and installing all-wheel-drive systems for large trucks.

This 26-foot 1953 Marmon-Herrington spent most of its life as a transit bus before its current owner purchased it for $100 in 1971. The conversion from bus to motorhome was done at a leisurely pace over a period of ten years, starting with the installation of a 1958 430-cubic-inch Lincoln gas engine and a four-speed automatic transmission. The owners have traveled all over the country in their motorhome and were among the first members of the renewed Tin Can Tourists. In appreciation of their dedication to classic RVs, Wilma and Bill Svec were inducted into the Tin Can Tourists Hall of Fame. Photographed in Camp Dearborn, Michigan.

Of all the bus conversions, the Scenicruiser is the undisputed king of the road. This twin-layered 40-foot leviathan originally served as the jewel in the crown for Greyhound Bus Lines. The first prototype Scenicruiser, the double-decker GX-1, touted as "the bus of tomorrow," was built by General Motors shortly after the end of World War II. Problems developed almost immediately, and engineers redesigned the bus and rolled out the second experimental model, the GX-2 (unit #001), in 1949. After some further modifications, Greyhound put in a $25,000,000 order for five hundred Scenicruisers (each unit cost $50,000) to be delivered in 1954 and 1955. The Scenicruisers, henceforth named the PD-4501 Super Scenicruisers, were delivered in 1954. An additional five hundred units were ordered for delivery in 1956 for a combined fleet of one thousand. One final unit, #1001, a prototype with a rear emergency door, was delivered to Greyhound in June 1956. The Scenicruisers ruled the highways for over two decades, and then they were retired by Greyhound in 1977 and 1978 and sold off, auctioned, or scrapped. Charter bus lines acquired a number of them, and a few were snapped up by private individuals who turned them into giant motorhomes.

Greyhound
Scenicruiser

Go Greyhound.
and leave the driving to us.

A 1954 REVOLUTION
BY DESIGN.

Converted Scenicruisers have been extremely popular with traveling bands and entertainers because of their ample storage space and durability. There are an amazing number of Scenicruisers still on the road despite the fact that they haven't been produced since the mid-1950s. This Scenicruiser #645 rolled off the assembly line in 1956. It has been retrofitted as a fully self-contained motorhome. The power plant is an 8v92 diesel pusher with 90 injectors that transmit power to the wheels via an HT 750 Allison transmission. An eight-kilowatt generator supplies ample AC power for three air conditioners and an electric water heater. Additional power is generated by roof-mounted solar panels that charge the 12-volt batteries. There are two water tanks, a 100-gallon fresh water reservoir, and a 100-gallon black water tank. Marty and Elaine Gross own the Scenicruiser. Photographed at the Flywheelers Park, Avon Park, Florida.

The award-winning interior is actually laid out on two different floors. The living room, located on the first level, consists of the driver and passenger seats (out of view), which swivel to become part of the living room, an overstuffed chair, and a small couch that converts into a twin bed. Other accoutrements include an entertainment center, cherrywood cabinets, skylight, tinted windows, and a quilted wall and ceiling panels.

The ample kitchen is lit with a large skylight that supplies all the illumination necessary during daylight hours. The cherry cabinets and accents are set off by the satin gray Corian countertops. A four-burner propane-fueled stove and a microwave take care of all the cooking needs, and a ceiling-mounted 13,500-BTU air conditioner supplies welcome cooling to the kitchen area.

The bedroom is separated from the rest of the living space by an accordion door. The clean lines and honey-toned oak cabinets and accents make the room warm and inviting. Darkly tinted windows and mini blinds provide privacy, while a dedicated heating and cooling system supplies the bedroom with its own controlled climate. The headliner is finished in the same pattern as the others, but it is made of a darker fabric more suited to a bedroom.

Bus conversions are not limited to the Americas. Numerous fine examples can be found in Australia. Affectionately called Oz by its residents, Australia is referenced in this bus's destination bar that cleverly states, "Gunaseeoz." This bus conversion was fabricated over a period of thirty months from a 1968 Bedford school bus. The bus was first manufactured in the UK in 1931. Its five-liter gasoline engine has been modified to run on clean-burning IPG (propane) fuel stored in two 180-liter tanks. Clearly outfitted for long journeys in the Outback, the motorhome is fitted with a full kitchen that features two refrigerators, a freezer, microwave, and range. A 400-liter water tank supplies ample water for the shower, continuous hot water system, and a washing machine. Other amenities include a full floating wood floor, two televisions, phone line, and backup camera. Of particular note is the front-mounted bull bar, also known as a roo bar, which fends off bounding marsupials. Gunaseeoz is owned by David Croft. Photographed at Sale, Victoria, Australia.

MOTORHOMES

Although lumbering mega mobile mansions are a common sight on our highways today, applying the words *motor* and *home* to signify a self-propelled home on wheels is a relatively recent development. The application of the words *motor home* to a vehicle wasn't common until 1958 when Raymond Frank and his teenage son, Ronald, built a motorized vehicle for use on family vacations. They dubbed it the Frank Motor Home. By the 1960s, the words *motor home* were a part of the lexicon of mobile America. Nowadays most RVers combine the two words into one word, *motorhome,* though dictionaries still break it up into two.

Motorhomes are divided into three classes: A, B, and C. Class C motorhomes were the result of the evolution of the slide-in truck campers of the 1950s. The problem with truck campers was that there wasn't any direct access to the camper from the truck's cab. Manufacturers solved the problem by removing the truck's bed and mounting a modified version of the truck camper directly to the chassis with the front open, which allowed egress between the cab and the camper body. Many bodies and frames were also extended to allow for a larger camper. Class B motorhomes are about the same size or smaller than Class C motorhomes, but they are adaptations of passenger vans like the Ford Econoline and Volkswagen Microbus. The camper is essentially built-in or inserted into the body of an existing van. Class A motorhomes are the big boys. They tend to have a profile similar to a transit bus. Although there are dozens of manufacturers of Class A motorhomes, most units are built on chassis and power plants supplied by truck and bus manufacturers. Prices for the top-of-the-line versions of these mansions on wheels often exceed $1,000,000.

The motorhome is one of the bookends that holds the history of RVing together. The other bookend is the diminutive camp car that first gingerly plied the tracks, trails, and roads over a century ago. Autocamping begat motor camping, which became trailering, which evolved into what we now call RVing.

Garry Grim owns this 1968 Travco. Photographed in Camp Dearborn, Michigan.

In 1958, Raymond and Ronald Frank, who lived in Brown City, Michigan, built a motorized all-weather recreational vehicle for family vacations. The father/son team's creation so enthralled the folks around Brown City that between 1958 and 1960 they constructed, using their barn as a factory, seven custom-made motorhomes for their friends. Their creations needed a proper name so they simply christened them the Frank Motor Homes. By 1961, Raymond and Ronald became managing partners in their own company. Raymond's wife, Ethel, took on the role of office manager and secretary.

In the first year of operation, the family churned out 160 units. The wood and aluminum bodies, which were mounted on a Dodge chassis, came in 20-, 23-, and 26-foot lengths and sold for between $6,500 and $7,300. In 1962, the Franks formed an alliance with Dodge, and thanks to the infusion of funds by the automotive giant, they were able to develop the tooling to fabricate an entirely new body made out of two huge 27-foot pieces of fiberglass. This streamlined design, which looked like an enormous version of the egg that holds Silly Putty, was a marked deviation from the boxy limited production house cars of the past. In order to further expand the Frank Motor Home's market appeal, it was decided that a more identifiable name would be needed and in 1963 the vehicle became the Dodge Motor Home. Two years later, the motorhome went through another incarnation when the company was sold to Detroit businessman Peter R. Fink who renamed it the Travco.

Through all the ownership and name changes, the quality and desirability of the Travco remained high, chiefly because of its rustproof fiberglass body and innovative features, like its optional sewage-incinerator system, the "Destroilet" gas-incinerator toilet that almost eliminated the need to empty holding tanks. There were problems to be sure: the 318-cubic-inch engine in the early models had to work very hard to go up any significant incline, there were stability issues because of the lack of anti-sway bars, and the low-slung body hampered tire changing. Eventually, a more robust 440 engine replaced the 318, other problems were corrected, and Travco became one of the most coveted motorhomes.

By the early 1970s, Travco experienced increased competition from other manufacturers, but the company failed to come up with new innovations to separate it from its competitors. Like all motorhome manufacturers, Travco's sales also plummeted as a result of the 1973 energy crisis. Travco still had alliances with Dodge/Chrysler, which unfortunately caused the company to suffer during Chrysler's financial woes in the late '70s. Travco Corporation finally ceased operations in 1979. In January 2004, the Travco's inspiration, the Frank Motor Home, was featured by *Playboy* magazine's 50 Inventions that Changed the World in celebration of the magazine's fiftieth anniversary. The list, which was a compilation of innovations in the last fifty years included the Big Mac, Pampers, Post-it Notes, and silicone augmentation devices.

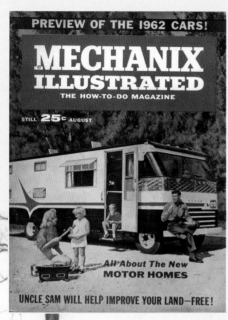

A Frank Motor Home graces the cover of the August 1961 issue of Mechanix Illustrated magazine. The revolutionary vehicle is featured in an article titled "Now You Can Live on Wheels."

This photograph, taken in 1958, is the only known photograph of the Franks's 27-foot trailer-like home on wheels. This first Frank Motor Home was built on a Ford chassis. The Franks switched to a Dodge chassis for their subsequent vehicles. Courtesy RV/MH Heritage Foundation.

While Winnebago was not the first company to manufacture self-propelled recreational vehicles, it is certainly the most well known. Indeed, for many people, the name Winnebago is synonymous with motorhome, just as Kleenex is synonymous with facial tissue and Jell-O is with gelatin dessert.

Winnebago got its start in 1958 when Forest City, Iowa, businessman John K. Hanson convinced a California trailer manufacturer to build a plant in Forest City. Like many fledgling companies, the manufacturer did not exactly have soaring sales, but within a couple years Hanson and four other local businessmen bought out and assumed control of the company. They renamed the company Winnebago Industries after the county where the factory was located. In the mid-1960s, Winnebago manufactured a full line of travel trailers and truck campers. Sales were steady and respectable, but disaster struck in the fall of 1964 when a ferocious fire raced through the wood-timbered Winnebago factory. After the smoke

This magazine advertisement is for a contest in which the lucky winner was to be be awarded a 1972 Winnebago Brave. The ad displays the motorhome with other recreation-oriented products to enhance its appeal.

had cleared, company officials assessed the situation and soon made plans to build a new modern facility, adapting the assembly line to build motorhomes, a move that would assure them a place in American history.

Thus, like the mythical Phoenix, Winnebago rose again—this time with a renewed strength. Their goal was to build a motorhome that would be accessible to the average American and to accomplish that they would have to price it at roughly half their competitors' prices, a task that they were able to carry out less than two years after the disastrous fire. The first units to roll off the new assembly line were produced under a contract with the Life-Time Industries of San Jose, California, but within a few months Winnebago was producing motorhomes under its own brand name in a body style that was more than a little similar to the Life-Time motorhomes. The first Winnebago, which was released in the spring of 1966, was simply named the F-19. A short while later, Winnebago introduced a 17-foot model, which sold for less than $5,000, and in the fall of 1966 the company introduced the 22-foot F-22. The public immediately embraced the boxy little RVs and by the end of the year the Winnebago was the best-selling motorhome in America.

Winnebago's fortunes soared in the heady times of the late '60s when it seemed that RV-related companies could do no wrong. By 1970, the company was listed on the New York Stock Exchange. In 1971, Winnebago Industries had the highest stock appreciation of any company on the New York Stock Exchange—462 percent. By the early 1970s, models had names like Brave, Indian, and Chieftain. The company weathered the tough times that were a result of 1973 energy crisis. In 1977, Winnebago produced its hundred thousandth unit, the first motorhome manufacturer to attain that lofty summit. The hundred thousandth vehicle was a luxurious 29-foot Elandan II. (Following the auto industry's lead, Winnebago started manufacturing models with made-up names. Elandan, it turns out, is the name of a type of tree that grows in the mythical land of Tamar.) In subsequent years, Winnebago Industries acquired other companies and increased its product line considerably. The company is still located in tiny Forest City, Iowa, and will always be known as the company that introduced the motorhome to the masses.

Ron and Shannon Westfall own this 1999 38-foot Winnebago Vectra Grand Tour. The couple won the 2002 and 2003 Slab City holiday lights contest. Slab City, America's most unusual free and informal campground, is located near Niland, California.

Gary Chamberlain owns this 1972 22-foot Winnebago Brave with a 360 V8 engine. Photographed at the Flywheelers Park, Avon Park, Florida.

GLASS HOUSES

In the late 1960s and early '70s, improvements in the fabrication of large pieces of molded fiberglass, a more outdoor-oriented lifestyle, and relatively cheap gasoline encouraged a number of companies to hop on the motorhome bandwagon. It seems that any company with sufficient facilities was plunking molded fiberglass shells onto truck chassis, declaring that they were a motorhome manufacturer. The energy crisis in 1973 drove most of these fledgling companies off the road, but not before they had created some unique fiberglass-shelled vehicles.

The Oasis Trailer Company gingerly stepped into the motorhome market with the introduction of this 1968 22-foot Oasis motorhome. The exact number of units manufactured by the Bellflower, California, company is unknown, but the VIN, #131, on this unit probably means that it was either unit 131 or 31. The Oasis is powered by a 318 Dodge engine and has a one-piece fiberglass top mounted on a Dodge M-300 chassis. One interesting aspect of the Oasis is its "tumblehome" design, a boat-building term that means it flares in the middle, which makes its bottom appear noticeably larger than its top. In this case, the tumblehome design results in a Darth Vaderesque profile. Jeff Hammers owns the Oasis. Photographed at the Deming Log Show Grounds, Bellingham, Washington.

This 26-foot 1972 Krager motorhome was built by the Krager Company in Winona, Minnesota. Winona's other claim to fame is that it is the birthplace of actress Winona Ryder. Like Ryder, whose family moved to Petaluma, California, when she was a small child, the Krager motorhome's tenure in Winona was very brief. At most, there were a few dozen units manufactured under the name Krager Kustom Koach, but despite their limited numbers they are very easy to spot thanks to their unusual front end. The modestly proportioned vehicle was powered by a generous 392 V8 International "Cornbinder" engine. The Krager's short wheelbase, high center, and noncorrosive fiberglass body made it more adaptable to backcountry roads than other bulky motorhomes. These qualities were meant to appeal to outdoorsmen and hunters. The unit was fully self-contained and was equipped with sleeping accommodations for four adults in bunk beds, rather than the standard two double beds. This lodging style definitely appealed to manly men. James Weaver Jr. owns the Krager. Photographed at the Deming Log Show Grounds, Bellingham, Washington.

Boat manufacturers have a long history of adapting their streamlined technology to motorhomes. Such is the case with this 20-foot 1970 Glastron
motorhome, manufactured by the Glastron Boat Company of Austin, Texas.
Like many other motorhomes of the era, the Glastron was equipped with a
318 engine and a fiberglass shell mounted on a Dodge M-300 chassis. The
Glastron's shell is, amazingly, just one piece of fiberglass hand fitted to the
safety-cage frame. This unit, thought to be the first of nineteen units manufactured, sold for $12,000 in 1970, a steep price when a similarly sized Winnebago
cost about half that amount. Gary and Lisa Sebastian own the Glastron.
Photographed at the Deming Log Show Grounds, Bellingham, Washington.

The interior of the Glastron is a study in compact functionality. Product
literature stated that the Glaston slept six comfortably in three double
beds, had a gas/electric refrigerator, 12-volt and 110-volt power, and
fully self-contained bathroom. By the 1970s, most travel trailers and
motorhomes had plastic veneers applied to particleboard, thus this
Glastron is a real gem since its interior is sheathed in red oak.

NEWELL

Like many innovative products, the Newell motorhome was born out of dissatisfaction with something else. In 1967, L.K. Newell traveled from Oklahoma to the Streamline factory in El Monte, California, to take delivery of a new Streamline motorhome. The Streamline company had been manufacturing travel trailers since the mid-1950s and had recently moved into motorhome manufacturing. Their Streamline motorhome was regarded as a top-of-the-line product, and Newell had high expectations for his acquisition. A couple weeks after taking possession of his new vehicle, Newell went back to the factory to have some modifications made. While the work was being done, he engaged in some lively conversations with the Streamline designers and suggested ways to improve the vehicle. During one of the heated conversations, someone remarked that if Newell thought he was so smart he should make his own motorhome. Newell took the challenge to heart and within a few hours struck a deal. He took charge of the motorhome-manufacturing arm of the Streamline company.

When Newell took possession of Streamline, he set out to build a motorhome from the ground up (the Streamline was built on a Ford chassis). His approach was to combine the best aspects of a motorhome with the best features of a bus. At first he tried using a Madson gas-powered bus chassis, but wasn't satisfied with its performance, so he designed and built his own chassis. Besides its profile, the most notable bus-like aspect of the Newell is the rear-mounted diesel "pusher" engine. This configuration allows for a lower floor and also for extra storage space. Today's custom-designed Newell motorhomes, known as Newell motor coaches, sell for upwards of $1,000,000. In 1970, the last Streamline trailer rolled out the door, but the Streamline motorhome, renamed the Newell, is still being manufactured today in Miami, Oklahoma.

Craig and Pat Leach are restoring this rare 30-foot 1969 Newell, which has a 454 gasoline engine. Photographed in Camp Dearborn, Michigan.

Bill Givens owns this 1977 Newell 39-foot diesel pusher. Previously he owned a 1971 Newell.
Photographed in Quartzsite, Arizona.

Although relatively few were manufactured, Barth motorhomes were produced from 1968 until the company was formally closed in 2001. The Barth name is well known among aficionados of high-end motorhomes. The company's history can be traced to Bob Barth, who owned the Beeline Trailer Company. In 1963, Barth left Beeline to form the Barth Trailer Company, which was founded on the principle of building quality all-aluminum travel trailers. At the time, many travel trailers and almost all mobile homes used a wood frame with aluminum sheathing. Barth produced his all-aluminum trailers in his Milford, Indiana, factory from 1963 until 1968 when he sold the company to Mike Umbaugh. Umbaugh, whose business experience was in banking and not RVs, saw the Barth Company as a solid investment opportunity. Immediately after acquiring the company, Umbaugh changed the focus from travel trailers (which he eventually phased out in 1970) to the growing motorhome market. Rather than try to compete with companies like Winnebago and GMC that produced a relatively affordable product, Umbaugh decided to produce a high-end product for more upscale buyers.

The Barth company never produced more than three hundred units per year, many of which were custom designed for the owner. Barth's sales plummeted during and after the 1973 energy crisis as did all motorhome manufacturers' sales. The company emerged from the crisis and altered its long-term vision by dedicating itself to manufacturing custom coaches designed for more commercial interests like mobile offices, medical support vehicles, dental labs, libraries, and remote TV production units. Throughout the 1980s and into the 1990s, Barth continued to manufacture motorhomes and specialized motor coaches but eventually ceased operations.

In 1998, the company's assets were sold to Keith Leatherman, owner of Leatherman Construction, who intended to revive the company. Leatherman spent approximately $500,000 retooling some of the manufacturing equipment and making plans to move the factory to Albion, Indiana, but due to a lack of orders, Leatherman officially pulled the plug on February 13, 2001. Thanks to Barth champion David R. Bowers, a wealth of Barth information can be found at www.barthmobile.com. A club for loyal Barth owners, the Barth Rangers, meets from time to time.

this is the year dreams come true

24   Tell 'em you saw it in TL!

BARTH INC.
MILFORD, IND.
46542
219-658-4147

An advertisement from the first year the Barth was produced depicts a happy family with what appears to be a 27-foot model. In the early years, in order to show off their all-aluminum exteriors, Barths were devoid of much paint. By the early 1980s, anodized aluminum panels added a splash of color, and a few years later most Barths were painted in an array of colors. Since many Barths were custom made, they tended to have highly individualized color schemes.

This early model is devoid of the distinctive back hump over the engine compartment that makes 1970s-era Barths easily identifiable. By the 1980s, Barth adopted a more traditional bus-like profile.

This is a 1974 30-foot model with the distinctive "Victoria" trunk. It sports a hearty 454-cubic-inch gasoline engine that ingests a copious quantity of fuel from its 120-gallon tank. Amenities include a six-kilowatt generator, rear stateroom, Pergo flooring, radar detector, customized roof package, and air horns. The entire ensemble rests on a Chevrolet/GMC chassis. The Barth is towing a 1937 Halsco Land Yacht, a magnificently intact unit from the golden age of the travel trailer. Jeff Hammers owns the duet. Photographed at the Deming Log Show Grounds, Bellingham, Washington.

This 1973 Chinook Class A Mobile Lodge, powered by a massive 413-cubic-inch Chrysler gas engine, was manufactured at exactly the wrong time, 1973. For years, Americans had been guzzling fuel at an alarming rate. In 1972, the average automobile got a mere 14.5 miles per gallon of gas. By the end of 1972, America's oil reserves were at critically low levels, and by the winter of 1973 there were widespread brownouts. For most Americans, the real crisis came in October 1973 when the Organization of Arab Petroleum Exporting Countries (OPEC) severely reduced their oil exports, which resulted in long lines at gas stations or simply no gas at all. The ultimate cruelty came during the Christmas season when President Nixon refused to turn on the National Christmas Tree's lights to save energy.

The Chinook pictured here may, according to the owner, have been the last one manufactured. After 1973, Chinook abandoned the manufacture of large RVs and started building Datsun- and Toyota-powered small Class C motorhomes. Eventually, Chinook went bankrupt. The Chinook name is now attached to another company that makes high-end Class A motorhomes. Mike and Deborah Babinetz own this 1973 Chinook. Photographed at Flywheeler's Park, Avon Park, Florida.

In the early 1960s, the first mass-produced motorhomes started appearing. Some of the early models look like a cross between a slide-in camper and a motorhome. These Class C motorhomes are constructed on a truck chassis. Fabricators ordered trucks without the traditional bed and added their own creation, a practice that is still done today. This rare 1963 Chinook is mounted on a Dodge chassis and is powered by a 318-cubic-inch engine. Owned by Walt Barnes. Photographed in Camp Dearborn, Michigan.

Certainly one of the most aerodynamic motorhomes ever made was the Rectrans (recreational transport). The Rectrans was the brainchild of Semon "Bunky" Knudsen who had served as president of the Ford Motor Company and had been a vice president at General Motors. Knudsen was looking for new horizons to explore and an opportunity arose when the White Motor Company hired him to build a motorhome to serve the growing RV market. Knudsen's first order of business was to hire famed stylist Larry Shinoda, who had designed the Corvette Sting Ray, the Z-28 Camaro, and the BOSS 302 Mustang. A second generation Japanese American (he and his parents were interred during World War II), Shinoda was recognized as one of the most brilliant minds in automotive aerodynamic design. When Shinoda arrived at the White facility in 1970, he was charged with the task of eking out 10 miles per gallon from a 10,000-pound motorhome.

Shinoda is credited as being the first person ever to use a wind tunnel to engineer a motorhome, a task he accomplished by carving a 1/25-scale model of his proposed vehicle and testing it at Fort Wayne University's wind tunnel. What resulted was a 25-foot long fiberglass shell mounted on a Dodge M350 chassis and powered with a 413-cubic-inch Chrysler industrial engine. It got 10.1 miles per gallon. Surprisingly the Rectrans could accelerate from zero to sixty miles per hour in eleven seconds. From 1971 until January 1974, there were approximately thirty-three hundred Rectrans built. Pictured here is a 1972 Rectrans Discoverer purchased new by its current owner in 1975. The motorhome had originally been built for a doctor but had never been delivered. At $17,735, it was the highest-priced model and had a number of custom features, including a "Thermosan," an ingenious sewage disposal system that pumped raw sewage through the exhaust system and incinerated it.

When the energy crisis hit in 1973, many motorhomes sat unsold and idle and gathered dust for months. By January 1974, production of the Rectrans ceased and the factory closed its doors. But the White Motor Company was spared a huge loss courtesy of a stroke of divine intervention when in March 1974 a lightning bolt hit the Brighton, Michigan, factory, burning it to the ground. The beleaguered company was able to collect on the insurance. Frank Canfield owns this 1972 Rectrans Discoverer. Photographed at the Flywheelers Park, Avon Park, Florida.

Discoverer-25. **Where no one has gone before.**

Depending on one's perspective, the 28-foot Daystar is either one of the ugliest motorhomes ever built or one of the most dynamic. The name Daystar, derived from Christian lore, refers to the bright star that guided the Magi. Information on this unique motorhome is very hard to come by since, reportedly, only sixteen were ever made. One source says Daystars may have been built by a religiously minded group, but nobody seems to know for sure. Daystar interiors were made of hand-carved teak by a yacht builder in Taiwan, and then they were shipped to Los Angeles where they were wired, plumbed, upholstered, and finally plunked down on a Dodge chassis. The finished Daystars supposedly carried a list price of $70,000. Jeff Hammers owns this 1975 Daystar. Photographed at the Deming Log Show Grounds, Bellingham, Washington.

Taking a page from the Starship Enterprise's mission statement, Rectrans promised to take their passengers beyond their humdrum existence. The sales brochure's florid prose transports readers into a different RVing dimension by referring to the dinette area as a unilounge and the driver's seat as a cockpit; it also dispenses with the term storage, inserting the jaunty nautical term stowage instead. Courtesy Frank Canfield collection.

FMC

The FMC motorhome has a very interesting lineage. FMC, an acronym for Food Machinery Corporation, got its start in 1883 when inventor John Bean developed an innovative insecticide pump. The name was changed from the John Bean Manufacturing Company to the Food Machinery Corporation in 1928 when the company got into the canning-machinery business. The company kept adding mechanized products, and eventually started producing amphibious vehicles for the military. In the late 1960s, during a lull in their military vehicle contracts, FMC turned its sights towards the burgeoning recreational vehicle market. By 1972, FMC had transferred personnel from its ordnance division and formally launched a motor coach division in Santa Clara, California.

Initial prototypes were 19 and 23 feet long, but neither one went into production. FMC settled on a 29-foot size, and the first one was completed in late 1972. The well-made and pricey coaches, which sold for between $27,000 and $54,500, or about the same price as an average home of that era, were popular among the upscale motorhome buyers. The FMC had a fiberglass body on an aluminum frame, mounted on a proprietary low-slung chassis and a rear-mounted engine. These features combined to give it excellent handling, a trait that appealed to racecar drivers Mario Andretti and Parnelli Jones, who each had an FMC. Tinseltown entertainers Clint Eastwood, Carol Burnett, Pat Boone, and James Brolin also owned an FMC. But the most famous person to have an FMC was CBS reporter Charles Kuralt, host of the popular news feature *On the Road with Charles Kuralt*. An FMC was last of Kuralt's six motorhomes. Fittingly, it is on public display at the Henry Ford Museum in Dearborn, Michigan.

The FMC coaches were only officially manufactured from 1973 until 1976. The 1973 energy crisis had already put a damper on the manufacture of all brands of motorhomes, which put the FMC coaches in a difficult position from the beginning. By 1975, FMC had a contract to produce the Bradley Fighting Vehicle. In September 1976, the FMC motor coach had reached a dead end and all of the tooling in the factory was converted to manufacturing M113 tanks. The final tally for the FMC was slightly more than one thousand units, approximately 135 of which were transit buses. About half of the transit buses were eventually transformed into motorhomes. It is estimated that about 600 FMCs are still registered and on the road. Despite their relatively modest numbers, FMC has two clubs, the FMC Club East and the FMC Club Southeast.

This FMC started out its life in 1975 as a transit bus in Denver, Colorado. After it had logged about 850,000 miles, it was put out to pasture. A few years later it was rescued, totally gutted, and converted into a motorhome. The present owners did a major restoration in 2000. They added a larger 75-gallon fuel tank, made numerous mechanical and cosmetic upgrades, and gave it a brand new paint job that was sympathetic to the original. The FMC is powered by a thumping rear-mounted Chrysler 440 Marine/Industrial gasoline engine that, thanks to a newly installed fuel-injection system, gets an impressive 8.25 miles per gallon. Jim Steinborn and Bill Rogers own the FMC. Photographed at the Deming Log Show Grounds, Bellingham, Washington.

The transit bus interior was completely gutted, and over a period of five years an entirely new interior was fabricated. Highlights include a full bath with tub, seating for six, and twin beds that link together to make a king-size bed.

FMC built only one motorhome model that was simply named 2900R, but different floor plans were available. Leif and Elinor Scott own this 29-foot 1975 FMC powered by a 440 Chrysler industrial engine. Photographed in Camp Dearborn, Michigan.

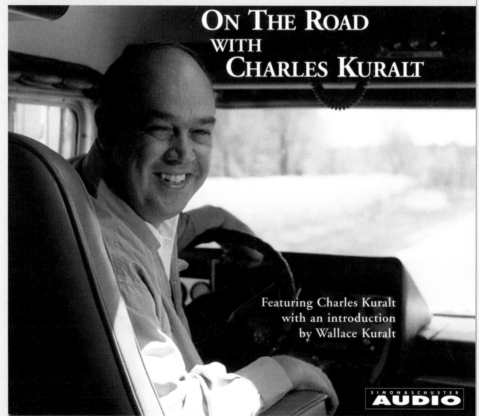

ON THE ROAD
WITH
CHARLES KURALT

Featuring Charles Kuralt
with an introduction
by Wallace Kuralt

SIMON&SCHUSTER
AUDIO

Famed broadcaster and motorhome owner Charles Kuralt traveled extensively in his FMC motorhome. His program, On the Road with Charles Kuralt, lives on thanks to videotape, DVD, and CD compilations of the programs.

GMC

GMC is the only major automotive manufacturer to produce its own motorhome from the ground up. For years, motorhome manufacturers had been plopping their creations on GMC's truck chassis, but by the early 1970s GMC decided it was time to manufacture their own custom-designed units. Initial design work on the GMC motorhome began in 1970 with an anticipated release date of 1973. The chief element of their creation was a front-wheel-drive design based on the successful Oldsmobile Toronado automobile, which incorporated a 455-cubic-inch gasoline engine coupled with a Turbohydramatic 425 transmission with torsion-bar suspension. The rear suspension utilized dual swing arms (one leading and one trailing) with a single air spring on each side. The combination of the front wheel drive, which eliminated a bulky drive train to the rear, and the suspension elements allowed for a low-slung vehicle with car-like handling and ride. A ladder chassis topped with an aluminum frame sheathed with aluminum and molded fiberglass body panels resulted in a ground-hugging vehicle that avoided the stability and handling problems of other top-heavy motorhomes. The molded fiberglass also allowed for a more streamlined design, a breath of fresh air during a time when motorhomes were becoming boxier every year.

The GMC motorhome debuted in May at the Transpro '72 trade show in Washington, D.C. A few months later, 1973-model-year vehicles rolled off the assembly line to general acclaim from the recreational vehicle community. Two models were offered, Model 230 (23 feet) and Model 260 (26 feet). The coaches were available in a motorhome configuration with a GMC-finished interior and a Transmode configuration, which was a bare coach sold to other RV manufacturers, like Avion and Coachman, that provided their

Richard and Jean Palmer own this 26-foot 1977 GMC Palm Beach model, powered by an Oldsmobile 455 engine. Topeka Graphics of Topeka, Indiana, custom painted it. Photographed in Camp Dearborn, Michigan.

own interior. As were other motorhome manufacturers, GMC was hit hard by the 1973 energy crisis, but it was a large enough company with sufficient resources to weather the storm. Eventually GMC officials determined that their factory space would be better utilized for building small trucks, and in November 1977 it was announced that 1978 would be the last model year.

In the six years of production, approximately thirteen thousand units rolled off the assembly line, of which about eight to nine thousand are still registered. Much of the endurance of the GMC can be traced to a legion of enthusiastic owners, the continued publication of the *GMC Motorhome News* and *GMC Motorhome Marketplace,* and the availability of parts from Cinnabar Engineering, which purchased all the motorhome property from GMC and negotiated a license to provide OEM parts for the vehicles.

Grand Slam motorhomes were produced by Champion Home Builders from the early 1970s until 1980. Champion introduced a similar vehicle, the Flagship-Champion, in the early 1980s, but that model met the same fate as the Grand Slam and the last Flagship rolled out the door in 1985. This 1979 23-foot Grand Slam is a quality motorhome constructed with a steel frame, aluminum sides, and a one-piece fiberglass top. The noncorrosive fiberglass and aluminum have served this motorhome well. Over twenty-five years after it was manufactured, thanks to the care given by its owners, the body is still in showroom condition. The power plant is a Dodge 360 engine, which transfers its energy via a three-speed automatic transmission to a 4.10 rear end with positraction. Owned by Ken and Lee Evensen. Photographed in Camp Dearborn, Michigan.

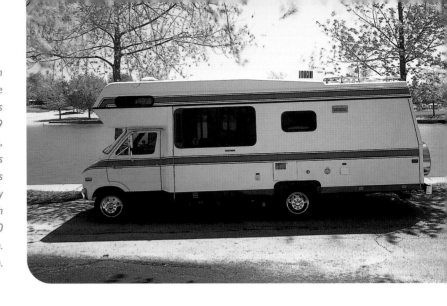

The Grand Slam's interior is truly an ode to the '70s. Almost nothing has been changed since it rolled off the assembly line. The interior is fitted with the original furniture covered in pussy willow fabric, and the period appliances are still in good working order. Only a modern television and a propane-powered lamp (out of view on the right) have been added by the owners. True to the '70s ethos, the wood-grained surfaces are actually a dark patinated contact paper—like plasticized material applied over particleboard. The only piece of real wood is the spindle at the center that holds up a cabinet. During the free-wheeling '70s, a number of manufacturers made what can only be described as pleasure palaces on wheels that sported plush upholstery, tinted windows, and '70s-era accessories, like lava lamps and assorted DayGlo accessories and fabrics. In the 1970s, when every vehicle sported a bumper sticker or two, one of the most popular with the RV crowd read, "If this camper's rockin', don't bother knockin'." The Grand Slam, while not a completely decked-out pleasure palace, does have deep pile carpet on part of the ceiling. A final touch and testament to the '70s is the afghan, made by the owner in 1974, which is draped over the sofa/bed combination.

This Silver Streak branded motorhome is a rare bird. Indeed, it may be the only roadworthy one in existence. Silver Streak was born in the flush travel trailer times following World War II when manufacturers scrambled to meet the surging post-war demand for recreational vehicles. The genesis of the Silver Streak Trailer Company occurred when investors Kenny Neptune, Frank Polido, and Pat Patterson bought the Curtis Wright Industries trailer company in 1949 and renamed it the Silver Streak Trailer Company. Based in El Monte, California, Silver Streak was essentially a boutique trailer manufacturer that never produced more than a few hundred units a year. But they were quality trailers and a surprising number of them are still on the road today.

The story goes that Silver Streak decided to enter the rapidly expanding motorhome market in the early 1970s but didn't actually produce any units until 1974, a date that unfortunately was during the energy crisis. Sales of all motorhomes plummeted during those depressing times, and Silver Streak didn't have the resources to establish much of a client base. Sources indicate that Silver Streak produced a dozen Class A and a dozen Class C motorhomes at most. All of the motorhomes that have been attributed to Silver Streak appear to have been custom made; no two are exactly the same.

This 1978 25-foot Class C motorhome is mounted on a Dodge M-400 motorhome chassis and powered by a Dodge 440 gasoline engine. The owner states that following a year of restoration he drove the motorhome and towed a 6,000-pound trailer from California to Ohio, averaging an impressive 11 miles per gallon. Owned by Jim Jarzebek. Photographed in Camp Dearborn, Michigan.

The interior of the Silver Streak is a perfect time capsule of 1978. Heavy dark brown, sculpted plush pile carpet covers the entire floor. The walls are sheathed in a faux-wood-grain plastic composite while other surfaces are covered in mottled yellow Formica. The generous eight-foot width allows for ample seating and includes a fully equipped kitchen and full bath. There is sleeping for four—the couch at the right converts into a bed and a queen-size bed (in back of the camera) is nestled into the space above the cab.

Without a doubt America's, most well-known motor coach traveler is sports commentator John Madden. Madden, who travels during the football season, started commuting between venues via motor coach in 1987. When Madden coached the Oakland Raiders in the 1970s, he traveled to games on airplanes, but he grew increasingly claustrophobic in the cramped quarters and abandoned traveling by air in 1979. From 1979 until 1987, he journeyed to distant locations on trains, and then in 1987 he acquired a converted Greyhound bus and has traveled by bus ever since. The most recent incarnation of the Madden Cruiser is a 45-foot Motor Coach Industries MCI E4500, sponsored by Outback Steakhouse.

The custom interior on the Madden Cruiser, fabricated by Klein Interiors Specialists of Nolensville, Tennessee, is finished in stained rosewood. The front lounge includes a sofa sleeper, and the adjacent galley features a convection microwave oven, three-burner glass-top electric stove, and side-by-side refrigerator. The dinette area, which doubles as a studio for his live radio shows, includes granite tops and accents. The bedroom office suite features a queen-size bed that slides to the side but can be centered for sleeping. The coach contains two baths, with an extra-large steam shower in the master bath.

The office area includes a built-in desk, computer, cell-phone system with three telephone lines, and a fax machine. Three Sony plasma televisions can be viewed from virtually any location in the coach. The focal point of Madden's communication apparatus is a KVH TracNet mobile high-speed internet system, which supplies a broadband connection even while moving along the highway. Courtesy KVH Industries.

Klein Interior Specialists, which fabricated the Madden Cruiser's interior, is one of America's premiere coach interior designers. Their clients include Nashville superstar Loretta Lynn, NASCAR driver Sterling Marlin, and country western singer George Jones. The two interior photographs are a progress photo and a finished photo of the fore section of the coach. The passengers are some of Klein's employees who are taking the coach on its maiden voyage. The bottom photograph illustrates the process of applying a "vehicle wrap." Vehicle wraps, which are similar to vinyl wallpaper, came into vogue in the mid-1990s with the advent of solvent inkjet digital printers. An accomplished wrapper can apply the vinyl to almost any surface in a fraction of the time it would take to paint a vehicle. If applied properly, the vinyl can be easily removed. Courtesy Klein Interior Specialists.

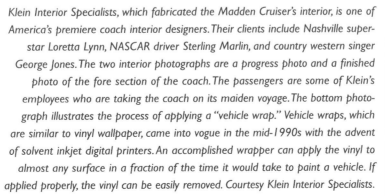

Anatomically improbable Barbie has had a number of motorhomes since her debut in 1959. She had a minivan and a variety of motorhomes and campers, including the Starlight Motorhome, Golden Dream Motorhome, Disco Motorhome, Barbie's Magical Motorhome, and a Star Traveler Motorhome in a GMC configuration. Barbie is allowed to travel with her gal pals but can only go on day trips with Ken. Despite Barbie's many wedding gowns and accessories and Ken's wedding tuxedo, the polymer pair have never been officially married, according to toymaker Mattel.

Always trendy and sometimes trendsetting, Barbie's clothing, accessories, companions, and even her motorhomes have changed with the times. The first motorhomes and campers, acquired by the blond icon in the early 1970s, were reminiscent of the boxy Winnebagos manufactured at the same time. The camper motorhome pictured above was manufactured in 1971 while the zoomy streamlined model to the left dates from 1996.

Popular Songs *magazine from August 1935 featured bawdy actress and songstress Mae West (1892–1980) on the cover. West started acting at age five, was doing burlesque under the name the Baby Vamp at age fourteen, and then starred in a play titled Sex that she also wrote, produced, and directed when she was an adult. The police shut the play down in 1926, and West was jailed on obscenity charges. Nevertheless, West moved to Hollywood and enjoyed a long, adventurous career. She started out life as a brunette, but spent the rest of her life proving that blonds have more fun.*

Motorhomes have come a long way since the first home-built house cars of the early twentieth century. Pictured on the left is a 1931 22-foot house car built on a Chevrolet truck chassis owned by silver screen sex-goddess Mae West. The vehicle, which has a six-cylinder engine, capable of achieving the blistering speed of 55 miles per hour, has an all-wood interior, two-burner stove, and kitchen sink. The vehicle sleeps four. The most interesting feature of Ms. West's home on wheels is the rear balcony, which provided her with a platform to address her adoring fans. In addition to her voluptuous figure, Mae West is known for her double-entendre quotes meant to confound the censors. Some of the most famous quotes attributed to her are, "Why don't you come up some time and see me?," "It's not the men in my life; it's the life in my men," and "Too much of a good thing is wonderful." When asked if censorship had affected her prosperity, she said, "I believe in censorship. After all, I have made a fortune out of it."

Looming over Mae West's house car is a 42-foot 2005 Monaco Dynasty, which sports a full kitchen with microwave, range, freezer/refrigerator, and washer/dryer. The master bedroom, which has a king-size bed, doubles in size via a slide out. The combination living/dining room also has a slide out that increases the room's size enough to accommodate two overstuffed swivel rockers, a sleeper couch, Corian-topped dining table, and complete home-entertainment unit with a 24-inch plasma television. RV historian David Woodworth owns both units. Courtesy Recreation Vehicle Industry Association (RVIA).

www.steelwheels4x4.com

PERSONAL VISIONS

As with every human endeavor, there are those who march to their own drummer. Whether they are poets or painters, athletes or attorneys, these highly creative folks seem to have been born with a different set of instructions. In the vehicular world, these off-kilter individuals are affectionately referred to as gearheads. They understand how mechanical devices work in the same way mathematicians understand numbers. Armed with acetylene torches, socket wrenches, duct tape, and determination, these mechanical wizards turn utilitarian RVs into art and architecture on wheels. Most of their fantastic fabrications start with a basic vehicle stripped down to the bare essentials of a chassis and power plant. What happens next is anyone's guess. Many times the builder can't truly predict the outcome. Some individuals work from plans but most only have the most basic of drawings and rely on their inner drummer to guide them along the winding path.

Belying its rugged exterior, Draco is a testament to compassion, love, and commitment. This one-of-a-kind full-time four-wheel-drive motorhome is the creation of Shahn Torontow of Victoria, Canada, who constructed it so his wife, Ross, an accomplished outdoor photographer, who was disabled by Lyme disease, could still go on backcountry photographic expeditions. The bones of Draco are an Oshkosh M-1000 Aircraft Rescue Fire Truck. Torontow stripped most of it down to the frame, leaving only part of the original cab.

Among the exterior structural elements are a wheelchair lift; hydraulic lifts to aid in stabilization and tire changing; 45-inch-high, 14-inch-wide tires; "Scorpion" coating over the exterior sheathing; and a winch with a 300-foot cable to get Draco out of almost any predicament. The unit is propelled by a 335-horsepower Caterpillar 3406A diesel-pusher engine that generates 100-foot pounds of torque. Mounted next to the engine is a eight-kilowatt diesel generator and an air compressor. Torontow completed the work on the vehicle in 2002. Photographed in Chico, California.

The cockpit command center has a multitude of knobs, gauges, and lights. Most unique are the controls for the nine exterior cameras, two of which are motion activated. There are also five perimeter cameras and two cameras mounted at the rear to assist the driver while backing up.

The compact and efficient living quarters adapts to a number of uses. Seen here is the view from the aft section. On the right is a seating area and table that converts into a bed. At the center top is a hatch with fold-down ladder that allows access to the roof. On the left is a large refrigerator, microwave, and three-burner stove. Ceramic dinner plates are held onto the steel plate wall by magnets, which are epoxied to the bottom of the plates. The interior is sheathed in aluminum tread plate and leather panels. Lighting is supplied by a combination of LED and halogen fixtures. Well-placed splashes of color, which are reflected in the polished metal, help to soften the industrial-duty fixtures and furnishings.

The shower, which is sheathed in ceramic tile with stainless inlays, has seven nozzles that each spray a fifth of a gallon per minute. Two people can take showers for ten days from the 140-gallon tank. The shower doubles as a sauna that heats up to over 100 degrees.

The aft section of the motorhome contains the bathroom on the right and a shower on the left. A macerator-type toilet liquifies waste, which is then rendered benign with a microbial compound. The end product can be pumped into the exhaust system where it is vaporized at over 1,000 degrees Fahrenheit. The sink, which is perched atop a curved vanity, is a stainless steel bowl with a hole in the bottom.

In the 1920s, clever folks adapted the automobile to almost any use. The Fulton Gospel Auto, which served as a wheeled church and a home, was the creation of evangelist John Fulton of Harrisburg, Pennsylvania. In the chilly winter months, John and his wife (who did the singing with accompaniment on a baby organ) journeyed to Florida where they traveled from city to city conducting open-air gospel meetings. The 23-foot-long, 10-foot-high, 8-foot-wide vehicle was equipped with a refrigerator, lavatory, cooking area, two Pullman beds, bookcases, and, for the natty camper, a clothes and hat press. At the rear of the Gospel Auto was a speaking platform that converted into a sleeping porch. According to a postcard handed out by the Fultons to promote their ministry, the Gospel Auto had 21 electric lights that ran on 54 Edison batteries and a 20-gallon water tank. The vehicle could carry 40 gallons of gasoline and 10 gallons of oil.

Evangelist Billy Leggette built this one-of-a-kind motorhome in Prince George, British Columbia, Canada, in 1962 and 1963. Leggette's design for his mobile home was apparently divinely inspired. In a flyer he distributed to his flock describing his evangelical mission, he wrote, "God gave me a mental picture of this design and dimensions while waiting before Him in prayer." The truck is a 1962 GMC 930 with a five-ton chassis powered by a modest 261-cubic-inch inline six-cylinder engine. Leggette and his wife traveled in their mobile mansion throughout Canada, the United States, and Mexico, spreading the gospel until his death in 1978 at age sixty-five. The present owner, Bill Coulson, rescued it from a farm property where it had been sitting for seventeen years. Photographed in Camp Dearborn, Michigan.

RVers are a friendly lot. Most have stories to tell and some have messages to convey. Such is the case with this mobile Fátima shrine that was spied next to the approach to the municipal airport in Calipatria, California. The shrine, which also contains a gift shop, is towed by a Prevost bus registered in Quebec, Canada. The couple piloting the ensemble would only say that they hailed from Europe and were on a religious mission.

Leonard Knight's religiously inspired camper started out its life as a 1951 Chevrolet ton-and-a-half dump truck. Leonard, who hails from Vermont, acquired the dump truck in 1983 in Gibbon, Nebraska, while he was on a spiritual quest. After he purchased the basic truck, he assembled the camper from bits and pieces of plywood he found near Mount Rushmore, South Dakota. He then made his way west to California. Eventually he settled in Slab City, California, an abandoned military base that is populated in the winter months by snowbirds from the northern climes. His first order of business was to decorate his plywood camper, which he did by ingeniously using window putty and liberally applying paint.

After finishing the decorations on the camper, Leonard moved on to bigger things. Leonard's spiritual quest seemed to take on a life of its own and the result has become one of the largest and most intriguing folk art creations in the world: Salvation Mountain (behind camper). Salvation Mountain is comprised of thousands of gallons of paint, hundreds of bales of hay, and an assortment of trees, telephone poles, and just about anything else that Leonard is given or finds. Although the messages embossed on Salvation Mountain are an assortment of quotes from the Bible, Leonard says that he wants to keep his message simple. "God is love," Leonard says. "That's simple enough for me."

In the mid-1990s, the American Visionary Art Museum in Baltimore, Maryland, featured Leonard's camper in one of its exhibits, but it is now back at Salvation Mountain for all to see.

Wendell and Edna Turner's 16,000-pound motorhome, complete with a porch, wood siding, faux-brick siding made of asphalt, and a chimney, is the quintessential cottage on wheels. Turner, who owned a trucking business in Oakland, Iowa, built this unique vehicle in 1952, years before companies began to formally manufacture modern motorhomes. The vehicle started out its life as a 1939 White truck which, after eleven years of service, was retired from Wendell's trucking company. Wendell stripped the truck down to the frame and created his unique home on wheels piece by piece without any formal plans. According to the owner, the whole assemblage is held together with over 1,500 screws.

In 1953, despite the skepticism of their friends and neighbors about the vehicle's roadworthiness, the Turners were ready to hit the road. From their maiden voyage to Texas, Colorado, and Wyoming to a 1975 trip to Branson, Missouri, the Turners logged over 100,000 miles throughout the West, Midwest, Canada, and Alaska. In 1976, the Wendell Turner motorhome was donated to Pioneer Village in Minden, Nebraska, where it is now permanently moored. Background photographed near Alma, Nebraska.

It's hard to say if the fore section of the Wendell Turner motorhome is a full-service cockpit or a drivable kitchen. The driver's seat folds down to allow access to the cockpit and curtains are rolled up and tied for driving and lowered at night for privacy. A Ford 390 Police Special, nestled below the kitchen table, replaced the original engine of the 1939 White truck. Gasoline for the hearty power plant is gulped from an 80-gallon fuel tank.

The most interesting feature of the motorhome's interior is a propane-powered fireplace. Control valves are recessed in the fireplace surround, which is sheathed in vintage linoleum. Directly behind the fireplace is a tidy bathroom, which is accessed easily from the bedroom. The bedroom has two rolling bunk beds that sleep four. A full kitchen is off to the right.

Horse-drawn gypsy wagons may be no more, but thanks to James Nelson, folks can have a modern-day version. By trade James is a sign painter and, according to his business card, moonlights as a brain surgeon and builder of gypsy caravans. James has created over a dozen gypsy wagons, some of which are mounted on conventional vans while others are stand-alone trailers. All of them are true to the gypsy spirit and have real stained-glass windows, rich wood interiors, and whimsical detailing. The tow vehicle in this photograph is a 2002, 12-passenger, one-ton Dodge van. After tearing off the roof, James constructed the shell of mahogany and pine so that it would be high enough to stand in but not too tall to cause instability. Photographed at the Flywheelers Park, Avon Park, Florida.

James has a workbench and printer inside the van so he can make signs while traveling. The ceiling is made of grooved plywood made to look like the slatted wood of the old gypsy caravans. In the back is a loft-like bed and a wonderful window that echoes those in old galleons. The interior is fitted with a heater, but there are no kitchen appliances and no sink. The caravan does have lots of baubles, beads, fabrics, and shiny objects. The gypsy motto, says James, is "gaudy is good."

The gypsy trailer, perfect for an itinerant fortune-teller, measures 7 feet by 10 feet and is constructed of mahogany and pine atop a steel frame. The same grooved plywood used in the van is used throughout the trailer's interior to simulate wainscoting. While the crystal ball, metallic fabrics, crystals, and candles did not come with the trailer, they were readily available at well-stocked gypsy emporiums.

This Besotes was built by Charles and George Besotes of Stockton, California. The brothers are best known as builders of finely crafted runabout boats that are now highly prized by collectors. In all, there were about two hundred Besotes runabouts manufactured from the end of World War II until the company's demise in 1973, but there was only one motorhome. The foundation of the 29-foot motorhome is a GMC chassis powered by a rear-mounted Chrysler V8 gasoline engine that delivers power to the wheels via a three-speed automatic transmission. The body of the Besotes has tubular framing covered with an aluminum skin. Except for the addition of a few modern conveniences, like a generator and air conditioning, the interior remains unchanged. Construction of the Besotes was started in 1967. Construction was completed and the vehicle was registered as a GMC motorhome in 1969. The current owners, Donn and Laurie Bosworth, acquired the vehicle in 2003. Photographed at Camp Richardson, Lake Tahoe, California.

One's first impression of this one-of-a-kind motorhome is that there has to be a story behind it, and indeed there is. The story goes that a General Motors fabricator was irritated because he felt that the GMC motorhome was misnamed as the foundation of the vehicle was really an Oldsmobile (a GM product, but one that had its own loyal following). He decided to build his own Oldsmobile motorhome. The bones of this unusual motorhome are a 1969 Oldsmobile Toronado front-wheel-drive automobile with a generous 455-horsepower engine. The motorhome's body is a 1967 Airstream Globetrotter, perfectly wedded to the Toronado by the addition of a stainless-steel panels, which were through bolted to the frame. The driver's compartment of the motorhome retains the Toronado's tilt steering wheel and unique rotating speedometer. Just about every gauge imaginable has been added to give the vehicle the look and feel of an airplane cockpit. Of special interest is the windshield, which came out of a 1953 Ford Stake Truck. In order to protect it from breaking, the builder provided the windshield with its own set of shock absorbers. The project was finally completed in 1982 after approximately four thousand hours of work.

After vehicle-enthusiast Greg Karam, who has owned twenty-two Oldsmobile Toronados, acquired the vehicle, he added a few of his own touches, including highlighting the tailpipes by installing two five-foot semitruck exhaust stacks sideways, adding a 1973 Harley Sprint on the back, and giving the Globetrotter a mirror-like finish by applying liberal amounts of jeweler's rouge followed by even more liberal amounts of elbow grease. Greg rechristened the vehicle the Airanado Airscream. Photo © Petey Faber with enhancement by Douglas Keister. Photographed near Charlevoix, Michigan.

When Jerry Walsworth retired from his job as a truck driver, he just couldn't part with the romance of piloting a huge mass of steel down the road. But after he and his wife Barb decided to pursue the RV way of life, they discovered there wasn't any motorhome that really fit their lifestyle. So, in 1992, they decided that the best thing to do was build a unique rig that suited them. They started with a 1969 Kenworth cab as the foundation and then built a conventional RV-type body with 2 by 2 wood framing sheathed in aluminum. The imposing vehicle, which was completed in August 1994, is 32 feet long (with 21 feet 6 inches of living space); 8 feet wide; and 11 feet 9 inches tall. When the Walsworths drove into campgrounds, they were often turned away because some snooty campground owners did not allow homemade "hippie buses" into their pristine RV parks. Jerry solved the problem by creating his own "KW" (Kenworth) logo. Their RV is now allowed into RV parks where it can mingle with more pedestrian RVs. Photographed in Hutchinson, Kansas.

The bedroom, located in the aft section, is sheathed in warm honey-toned oak paneling. The tidy space houses a queen-size bed, his and her closets, and a collection of Beanie Babies on their own special lighted stage. Mini blinds provide requisite privacy.

The KW's mid-ship area is bathed in a warm glow thanks to the maple plywood, which sheathes the walls and floor. The tidy living room contains many souvenirs from the Walsworths' travels, including a Native American rug that covers the convertible couch.

What appears to be some sort of intergalactic transportation device is actually a combination motorhome/limousine that was the brainchild of Finnish immigrant Antti Rahko. Antti, who is a mechanic by trade, welded two 1983 Mercedes station wagons together in 2000 and then got to work accessorizing his creation. Highlights of the 30-foot turbo-diesel vehicle are a flying saucer–like, wind-activated generator that supplies energy for the multitude of lights; two driven axles to facilitate tight turning; mirrors on the rear doors so passengers can see where they've been; a refrigerator; stove; patio lights; a Finn-jet side-mounted exhaust that belches diesel smoke; and miscellaneous parts salvaged from over forty different vehicles.

When configured as a motorhome, the Mercedes sleeps two, leaving ample room for garage-sale finds Antti and his wife pick up during their travels. An extra large refrigerator accommodates the gallons of blueberries the couple picks up on their annual trip to Canada. By the spring of 2005, the vehicle had logged 235,000 miles. Photographed at Lake Worth, Florida.

Inside a small glass window, American and Finnish flags wave in a breeze generated by a small built-in fan. A clutch of projectile-like taillights cap what is certainly Antti's credo, "Thank you, Lord, for humor."

Ample illumination on this monument to incandescence is provided by nine headlights, which are a combination of European and American Mercedes units. A ring of seventeen mirrors, which circle the windshield, facilitates views to the rear.

This van on steroids is another fanciful creation of Finnish immigrant Antti Rahko. Antti fabricated this motorhome stretch van in 1995 from a standard issue 1984 GMC van by adding two more driven axles and more than doubling the length to 30 feet. The total assembly, which weighs in at 16,400 pounds, utilizes parts from over three dozen different vehicles. The van, which sleeps two, is a completely self-contained five-room home on wheels. The "rooms," which include a driving compartment, eating area, kitchen, bedroom, and bathroom, are fitted with a variety of comforts, such as an electric range, refrigerator, microwave, grill, toilet, entertainment unit, three spare tires, 140 light bulbs, and two air conditioning systems.

But, the pièce de résistance is the tiny 8 by 5–foot trailer tagging along behind the van, which contains a necessity of life for any self-respecting Finn—a sauna.

The two-person sauna, which can reach a blazing 220 degrees, is fired by propane. Although sauna aficionados prefer to jump into a cool lake or stream after getting properly superheated, this sauna also contains a shower to cool off. And to accommodate the need for a sauna on long nonstop journeys, both sauna and shower are completely functional when the van is in motion.

It seems fitting that this monster motorhome is from Australia, the same country that gave us Mad Max and The Road Warrior. The owners dubbed the vehicle the WORT (Weird Off Road Truck), or the Wothahellizat. The motorhome goes one step beyond the already extreme 4 by 4s: it is a six-wheel drive (6 by 6) and can go places that even 4 by 4s fear to tread. Its lineage can be traced to the Australian Constructed Cab Over vehicle (ACCO), an army vehicle that became a fire-brigade vehicle before landing in the possession of Australian photographer Rob Gray.

Rob toiled for over three years, from late 1997 to early 2001, to turn the industrial vehicle into a comfortable go-anywhere motorhome. He stripped the truck down to the frame, had a truck shop add a few feet to the frame, and then got to work constructing the aluminum-clad steel-frame body. The final result is a sight to behold. Statistics can hardly begin to tell the tale: six 1200 by 20 tires, 130-gallon diesel fuel tank, 1,125 miles on a fill-up, 200 gallons of water, and a 20,000-pound winch to extricate the Wothahellizat out of just about any situation. The fully self-contained interior is fitted with a refrigerator, gas cook top, microwave, and "expand-a-loo" toilet that opens out for use and then retracts to allow passage through the hallway. Roof-mounted solar cells assist battery charging, and a 3,300-watt inverter provides alternating-current when needed. Without a doubt, the most interesting feature is the foldout observation deck that affords splendid views and a great platform for taking wildlife photographs.

Rob and his wife, Chris, quit their jobs in 2000 and now spend most of their time traveling and photographing throughout Australia. Exterior photographed at Blowholes, Western Australia; interior photographed at Perlubie Beach, South Australia. Photos © Rob Gray.

"Trailer meets bus and motorhome" emerges. This bus-like vehicle, assembled in the early 1970s, is actually a 1954 Spartan Imperial Mansion trailer wedded to a 1970 GMC bus chassis. The builder, Dr. William Shultz of Bishop, California, had plans to manufacture these vehicles in quantity since there were (and still are) a number of the superbly built Spartan trailers moldering away on farms, ranches, and in backyards. His dream never came to fruition, but thanks to Rod and Phyllis Johnson of Issaquah, Washington, this interesting silver mansion continues to roll down the road. Photographed at the Deming Log Show Grounds, Bellingham, Washington.

This exceptional RV is a marriage between two iconic camping vehicles—an Airstream trailer and a Volkswagen van. The chassis is a 1959 Volkswagen van. Mounted atop the VW is a 16-foot 1949 Airstream Wee Wind travel trailer, which at the time was the smallest Airstream ever made. The Wee Wind had one major design flaw: a lengthwise spine of tubular steel to support the floor members and ribs that led to problems with torsional flexing. Merging the Wee Wind to the ladder-like frame of the VW solved that problem. The ensemble was the creation of an engineer who had a background in the aviation industry.

The current owner, Barry Weiss, who has owned a number of vintage trailers and motor coaches, is used to having people pull up beside him for a closer look while he motors down the road. Understandably, he was a little perplexed when he noticed people scattering when he drove the Wee Wind on the highway. He later found out that sometimes people mistake it for a run-away trailer and take evasive action. Photographed in Los Angeles, California.

This 1940 Futurliner is a tribute to the popularity of streamlining in the 1930s and the dedication of the people who participated in its restoration. The genesis of the Futurliner lies with one Charles F. Kettering, a General Motors research vice president who was responsible for a number of technological breakthroughs, such as the commercial electric self-starter, ethyl gasoline, and the diesel-electric locomotive. Inspiration struck when Charles, also known as Boss Ket, attended the 1933 Chicago World's Fair. Admiring the GM exhibits, he wondered if there was a way to enhance the impact and visibility of those exhibits by taking them on the road in some sort of public display. He took his idea directly to the president of GM, Alfred P. Sloan Jr., who gave him approval to build his proposed traveling exhibits.

What resulted was the Parade of Progress, a traveling exhibition housed in eighteen vehicles and looked over by a staff of forty to fifty people. The stars of the show were eight enormous streamlined vans, each mounted on a 223-inch truck chassis. The finished vehicles were 33 feet long, 8 feet wide, and 11 feet 7 inches tall. The drivers sat high atop the vehicle in a cockpit-like chamber. The driver's head was a full 10 feet above the roadway, which, according to reports, resulted in an unnerving experience for the driver while going beneath underpasses. The vehicles and their exhibits were extremely successful, so much so that in 1940 the original eight Streamliners were replaced by updated versions dubbed Futurliners. By the time the updated Parade of Progress hit the road in 1941, the dark clouds of war were looming. After the Pearl Harbor attack, the traveling exhibition was moved to a warehouse in Ohio where it remained until 1953.

In 1953, the Parade of Progress was revamped and new space-age exhibits were added on subjects like jet propulsion, the atom, the atmosphere, and stereo. But the public's growing fascination with the relatively new medium of television stole a lot of attention from the Parade of Progress, and the Futurliners were retired for good in 1956. Over the next few decades, some of the Futurliners found new life as advertising vehicles for a variety of companies, but eventually all of them fell into disuse.

Nine Futurliners are still accounted for, but only one (pictured) has been completely restored to its former glory. Futurliner #10 is owned by the National Automotive and Truck Museum (NATMUS) in Auburn, Indiana. It served for a time as a rolling billboard for a Cadillac dealership before it was acquired by NATMUS. The spectacular restoration of this Futurliner was undertaken from 1999 until 2005 by a group of dedicated men and women volunteers in Zeeland, Michigan. What the crew accomplished, under the supervision of retired GM plant manager Don Mayton, is nothing short of miraculous. Photographed in Zeeland, Michigan.

Side view of the restored Futurliner #10.

Futurliner #10 in 1998, prior to restoration. Courtesy Al Batts.

ACKNOWLEDGEMENTS

What a wonderful gaggle of folks! RVers are some of the friendliest people on Earth. It might be because they can simply move at will. Unlike the rest of us who are permanently or temporarily moored in our bolted-down communities, they take the bumps in the road of life a little more serenely. If RVers are a friendly lot, that friendliness increases exponentially for owners of vintage and classic RVs. These folks have an obvious appreciation for the history and preservation of all things ancient. If it weren't for the following list of generous and likeable souls, photographing and researching *Mobile Mansions* simply would not have been possible:

John Agnew

Cindy Ainsworth, National Automobile Museum

Jeff Anderson, Sloane Museum

Mike and Deborah Babinetz

Walt Barnes

Al Batts, Futurliner

Stan and Josie Biega

Doug Boilesen

Forrest and Jeri Bone

Donn and Laurie Bosworth

David Bowers, Barthmobile

Brad Boyajian

Norm Brauer, Norm Brauer Productions

Randall Briggs, The Stray Hound

Josh Brown

Ralph Burcar

Wallace Burch

Ray Bystrom

John Agnew

Charon

Bus Michael (on right) and two groupies

The Tin Can Tourists

Frank Canfield

Gary Chamberlain

Charon

Jim Cleveland, Pioneer Village

Richie Clyne, Imperial Palace

Fred and Peggy Sue Cochran

Virginia Coffman

Linda and Don Coolich

Bruce Coons

Bill Coulson

Julianne Crane, *The Spokesman Review*

David Croft

John Croft

Art Dietrich and Heidi Hough

Ken and Lee Evensen

Patrick and JoAnne Ewing

Ken and Petey Faber

Bill and Denise Fletcher

John and Dot Flis

Forrest Gist

Bill Givens

Rob Gray

Garry Grim

Marty and Elaine Gross

Dick and Peg Hale

Checker Larry Hamlin

Jeff Hammers

Kelli Harms, Winnebago Industries

Kathey and Vern Heaney

Stephen Heinrichs

John and Dot Flis

The Futurliner Crew

Norm and Marion Helmkay

Al Hesselbart, RV/MH Heritage Foundation

Art Himsl

Amanda Holder, Steinbeck Museum

Win Howard

Jim Jarzebek

Michael Jernigan

Rod and Phyllis Johnson

Buck Kamphausen

Karla, Rob, and Paul, RVTV

Zane Kesey

Henry Kimmel

Jay Klein, Klein Interior Specialists

Leonard Knight

Craig and Pat Leach

Rich Luhr, *Airstream Life* magazine

Ken Mantz

Skip Marketti, Nethercutt collection

Vince Martinico, Auburn Trailer collection

Sara Mauck—RVIA

Don Mayton, Futurliner

Theresa McDevitt, Indiana University of Pennsylvania

John McMullen

Richard Menzies

John and Mary Jane Merschdorf

John Miller, Firestone Tire & Rubber Company collection

Helge Mononen

James Nelson

Milton Newman

Jim Orr, Henry Ford Museum

Richard and Jean Palmer

Tom Patterson

Doug Payne

Barbara and Paul Piché

Joe and Gail Pirri

Virjillio Ponce

Terry Prentkowski and Bernie Stuckey

Jim and Sheri Reddy

Antti Rhako

Gary Rodgers, Henry Ford Estate

Dianne and Chuck Schneider

Laura Schweitzer

Richard Menzies and the Winnemucca nine

Shahn Torontow

James Nelson

Leif and Elinor Scott

Chuck and Donna Simpson

Jess Smith

Brian and Joyce Smithson

Sstoz Tes, Center for Steinbeck Studies at San Jose State
University

Jim Steinborn and Bill Rogers

Wilma and Bill Svec

Sarah Templin, American Visionary Art Museum

Shahn Torontow and Ross Johnson

Travis Travnikar

Leah Tye

Bill W. and Dr. Bob

Duke Waldrop

Jerry and Barb Walsworth

Mike Ward, *RV Life* magazine

Chris Watson, KVH Industries

Barry Westfall

Ron and Shannon Westfall

Don Wheat, Alaskan Campers

Bob and Ann White

Wicked Campers

Ron Wiebe

David Woodworth

Michael Wright

Special thanks also go to the groovy guys and gals at
Gibbs Smith, Publisher; my perfectly swell agent,
Julie Castiglia; and most of all my wife, Sandy.

Wilma and Bill Svec   *Checker Larry and Zydeco*

SUGGESTIONS FOR FURTHER READING

Belasco, Warren J. *Americans on the Road: From Autocamp to Motel, 1910–1945,* reprint ed. Cambridge, Massachusetts: The Johns Hopkins University Press, 1997.

Brauer, Norm. *There to Breathe the Beauty.* Dalton, Pennsylvania: Norm Brauer Publications, 1996.

Burkhart, Noyes et al. *Trailer Travel: A Visual History of Mobile America.* Layton, Utah: Gibbs Smith, Publisher, 2002.

Gellner, Arrol, and Douglas Keister. *Ready to Roll: A Celebration of the Classic American Travel Trailer.* New York, New York: Viking Studio, 2003.

Keister, Douglas. *Silver Palaces.* Layton, Utah: Gibbs Smith, Publisher, 2004.

Long, John D., and J.C. Long. *Motor Camping.* New York: Dodd, Mead, and Co., 1926.

White, Roger B. *Home on the Road: The Motor Home in America.* Washington, D.C.: Smithsonian Books, 2000.

Wood, Donald F. *RVs & Campers 1900–2000: An Illustrated History.* Hudson, Wisconsin: Iconografix, 2002.

RESOURCES

CLASSIC AND VINTAGE MOTORHOME BRANDS

ALASKAN
www.alaskancamper.com

BARTH
www.barthmobile.com

FLXIBLE
www.flxibleowners.org

FMC
www.steinborn.org/jim/fmc

FUTURLINER
www.futurliner.com

GMC
www.gmcmotorhome.com
www.gmccoop.com

GREYHOUND
www.scenicruiser.com
www.strayhound.com
www.pd4501.com

NEWELL
www.newellcoach.com

TRAVCO
www.mytravco.com

ULTRAVAN
www2.onu.edu/~kwildman/ultraVan.html

VIXEN
www.stannerair.hypermart.net

WINNEBAGO
www.winnebagoind.com

MEDIA IN THE UNITED STATES AND CANADA

BUS CONVERSIONS MAGAZINE
www.busconversions.com

CAMPING LIFE
www.campinglife.com

ESCAPEES MAGAZINE
www.escapees.com/magazine.asp

FAMILY MOTOR COACHING MAGAZINE
www.fmca.com/fmcmag

GYPSY JOURNAL
www.gypsyjournal.net

HIGHWAYS MAGAZINE
www.goodsamclub.com

MOTORHOME
www.motorhomemagazine.com

POP UP TIMES MAGAZINE
www.popuptimes.com

DEALERS, SUPPLIERS, AND REPAIR

CLUBS AND ORGANIZATIONS

RV JOURNAL
www.rvjournal.com

RV LIFE
www.rvlife.com

RV TIMES
www.rvtimes.com

RVTV
www.rvtv.ca

TRAILER LIFE
www.trailerlife.com

WORKAMPER NEWS
www.workamper.com

OUT WEST NEWSPAPER
www.outwestnewspaper.com

ADOHEN SUPPLY CO. (ROOF VENTS)
members.aol.com/fantasticvent

AIRSTREAM DREAMS
www.airstreamdreams.com

ARIZONA RV SALVAGE
www.azrvinc.com

BD ENGINE BRAKES
www.bd-vfi.com

CAMPING WORLD
www.campingworld.com

DOMETIC (RV APPLIANCES)
www.dometic.com

FUNKY JUNK FARMS (VINTAGE RV RENTAL)
www.funkyjunkfarms.com

IOWA BOYS (VINTAGE RV SALES AND RENTALS)
www.iowaboys.com

RV COLLISION CENTER
www.rvcollisioncenter.com

VINCE MARTINICO
(VINTAGE RV COLLECTION; RENTALS AND SALES)
www.auburntrailercollection.net
bigyellowt@yahoo.com

FUN ROADS (EXHAUSTIVE LIST OF CLUBS, ORGANIZATIONS, AND OWNERS)
www.funroads.com/club/viewClub.jhtml

TIN CAN TOURISTS ORGANIZATION
(PREMIER ORGANIZATION FOR OWNERS OF VINTAGE RVS)
www.tincantourists.com

MUSEUMS

NATIONAL AUTOMOBILE MUSEUM
www.automuseum.org

NETHERCUTT MUSEUM
www.nethercuttcollection.org

PETERSEN AUTOMOTIVE MUSEUM
www.petersen.org

PIONEER VILLAGE
www.pioneervillage.org

RV/MH HERITAGE FOUNDATION, INC.
www.rv-mh-hall-of-fame.org